THE *Mural* AT THE *Waverly Inn*

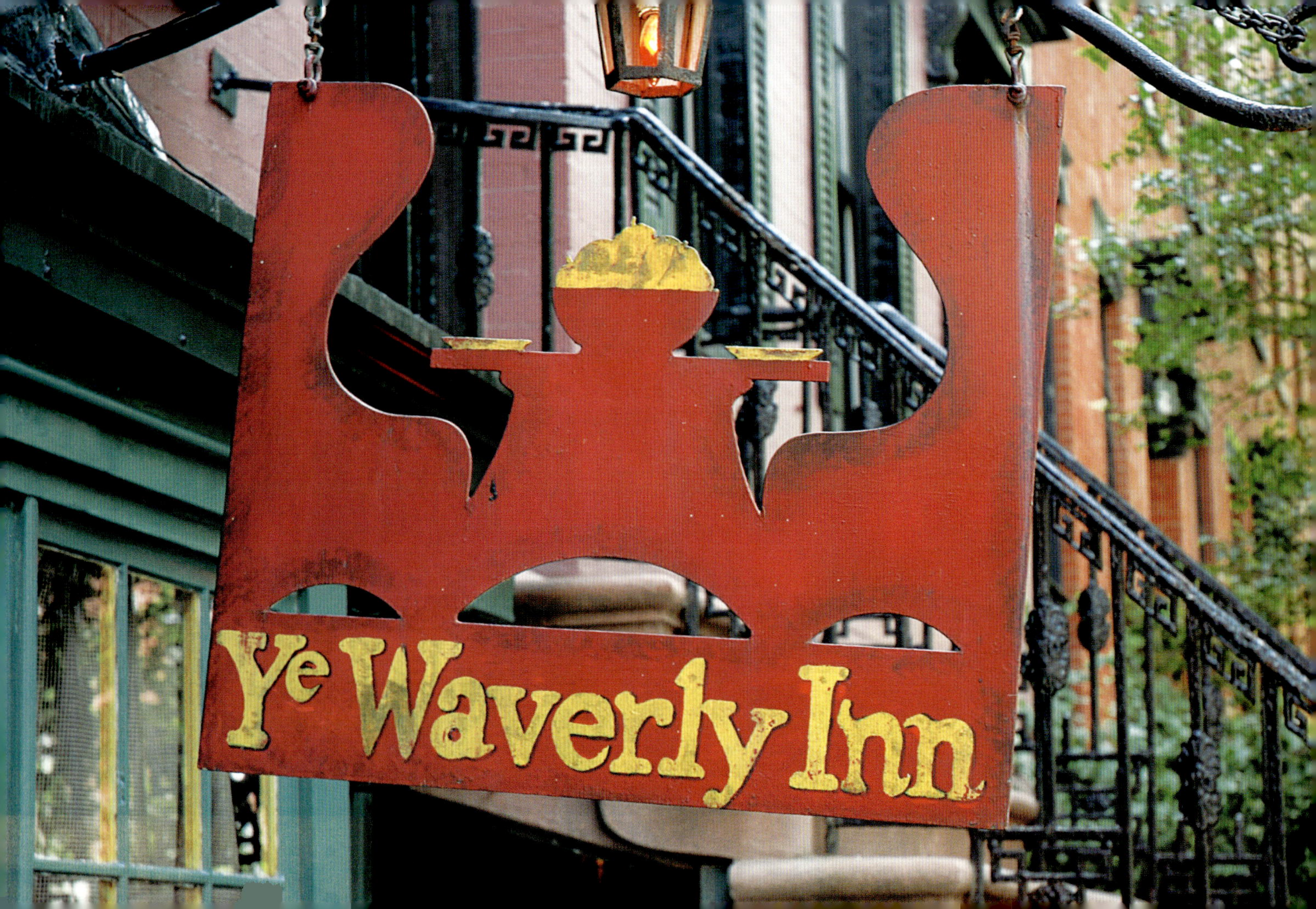
Ye Waverly Inn

Edward Sorel

THE *Mural* AT THE *Waverly Inn*

A Portrait of Greenwich Village Bohemians

Text by Dorothy Gallagher ✧ *Introduction by* Graydon Carter

Design by Walter Bernard

PANTHEON BOOKS, NEW YORK

 Published in the United States by Pantheon Books, a division of Random House, Inc., New York, and in Canada by Random House of Canada Limited, Toronto.

Pantheon Books and colophon are registered trademarks of Random House, Inc.

Based on original artwork by Edward Sorel that appears as a mural in the Waverly Inn, New York.

Library of Congress Cataloging-in-Publication Data
Sorel, Edward, [date]
The mural at the Waverly Inn : a portrait of Greenwich Village bohemians / Edward Sorel ; text by Dorothy Gallagher.
p. cm.
ISBN 978-0-307-37731-9
1. Sorel, Edward, [date]. 2. Mural painting and decoration—New York (State)—New York. 3. Authors, American—New York (State)—New York—Portraits. 4. Artists—New York (State)—New York—Portraits. 5. Bohemianism—New York (State)—New York—History—20th century. 6. Greenwich Village (New York, N.Y.)—Intellectual life—20th century. 7. Waverly Inn (Restaurant). I. Gallagher, Dorothy. II. Title.
ND237.S6343A4 2008 759.13—dc22 200800933

www.pantheonbooks.com
Printed in Malaysia
9 8 7 6 5 4 3 2 1 First Edition

*This book is for Katherine Hourigan,
who, after seeing the mural,
insisted on turning it into a book.*

*With gratitude from
Edward Sorel
and Dorothy Gallagher*

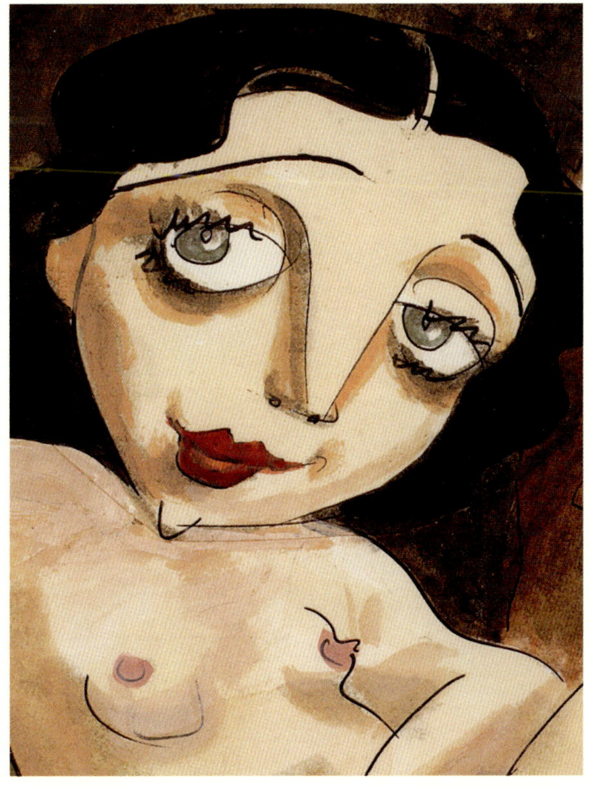

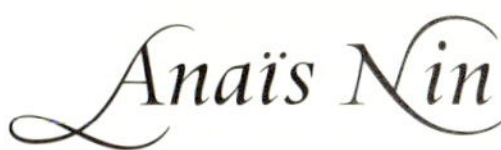

Anaïs Nin

ANAÏS NIN WROTE DREAMY, poetic novels and pornography, too, but only when she needed the money. Mostly she is remembered for her diaries. She wrote everything down, thirty-five thousand pages by the time she was finished recording her thoughts about herself and her life. She wrote so constantly that Anatole Broyard thought she must have also written her own face, so precisely did she paint her mouth and redraw her eyebrows.

Whether she was in Paris or Greenwich Village, Anaïs slept with everyone, and of course she wrote that down, too. It was rumored that her lovers included Henry and June Miller, Gore Vidal, Otto Rank, James Agee, Lawrence Durrell, her own father (but only when she was in her thirties), plus her two husbands, to whom she was married simultaneously. Some skeptics thought that she didn't sleep with as many people as she said she did, but even so.

Anaïs was sometimes called "The Madonna of the Clitoris." Later in her life, she became an icon of the feminist movement. She also coined many aphorisms, among them the useful "Good things happen to those who hustle."

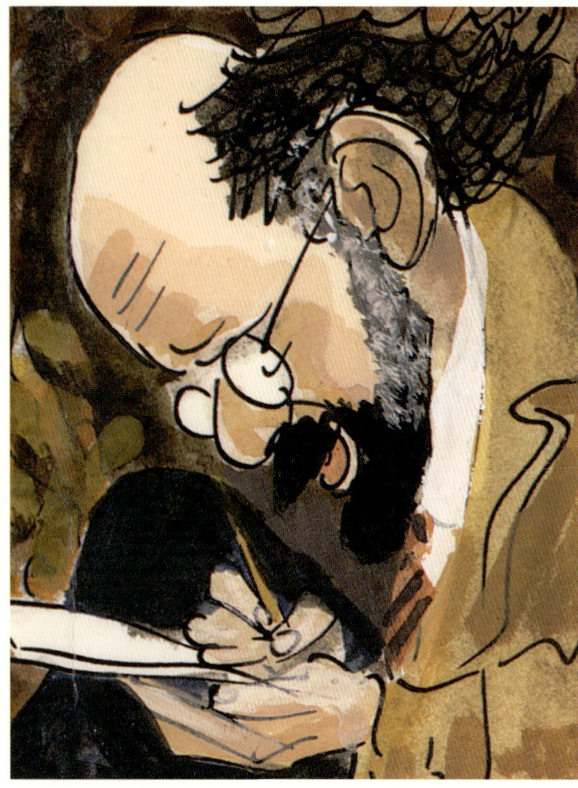

Allen Ginsberg

NAOMI, ALLEN GINSBERG'S MOTHER, was a communist. She went mad, but one thing had nothing to do with the other. Allen's father, Louis, was a poet.

Allen went to Columbia University, where he fell in with a pretty weird bunch of guys: Jack Kerouac was weird, so was William Burroughs. Later, Burroughs killed his wife, but it was an accident; Allen's friend Lucien Carr killed somebody, too. Herbert Huncke, another pal, was a Times Square hustler. This group of guys, including Neal Cassady, became the Beats, icons to a generation, even though no one actually knew what "Beat" meant. They drove around the country a lot, writing everything down and searching for . . . something. Sex and drugs were important to their work; also important was talking all night. "Howl" is Allen's most famous poem. He also wrote a poem called "America," which contains the lines: *America stop pushing I know what I'm doing. . . . America I'm putting my queer shoulder to the wheel.*

Eventually, Allen gave up drugs. He studied with gurus and became a guru himself. When he was in the Village, he lived on East Seventh Street. When Allen was inducted into the American Academy of Arts and Letters, Kurt Vonnegut noted of himself and Allen, "If we aren't the establishment, I don't know who is."

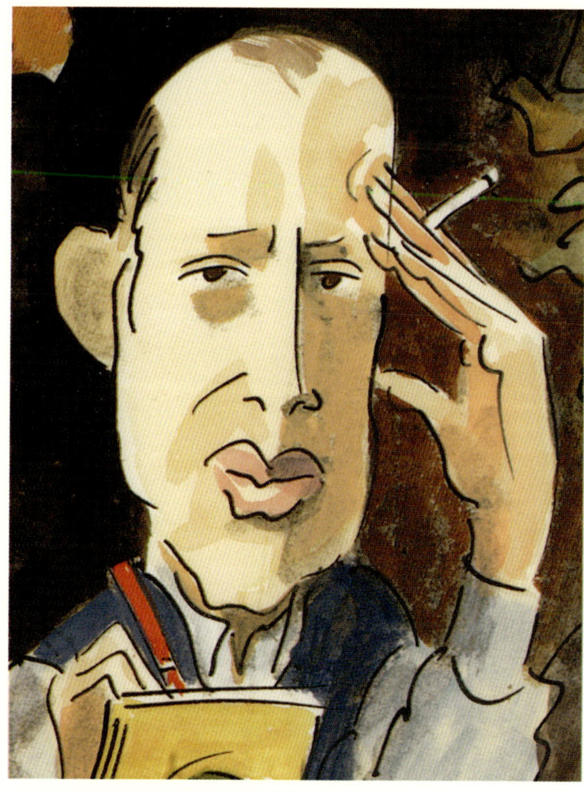

e. e. cummings

LIKE MANY WRITERS OF HIS TIME, Edward Estlin Cummings—"Estlin" to his friends, "e. e." to his readers—had advanced literary notions (i.e., not using Capital Letters). Estlin was Cambridge born and Harvard bred. His father had high hopes for him, but Estlin's ambitions were to write, to paint, to lose his virginity, and to live in the Village. In time, he did all those things in the Village, except for the lost-virginity part, which he dealt with in France.

Estlin was very susceptible to women. Realizing this, women treated him badly. He had three wives. His first wife soon left him for another man. Of his second, Estlin wrote, "She was a woman upon whom many men might go, as if she were a ship." This same wife referred to him as "my puny husband," among other aspersions on his virility. Finally, Estlin married a third wife, with whom he was very happy.

Estlin developed some unfashionable political views; he thought that President Roosevelt was taking orders from Moscow and that Jews, whom he called kikes, ran the country. For almost forty years, Estlin lived at 4 Patchin Place, across the courtyard from where Djuna Barnes lived. He painted by day, wrote poems at night, and grew old. "*Life's not a paragraph,*" he wrote, "*And death i think is no parenthesis.*"

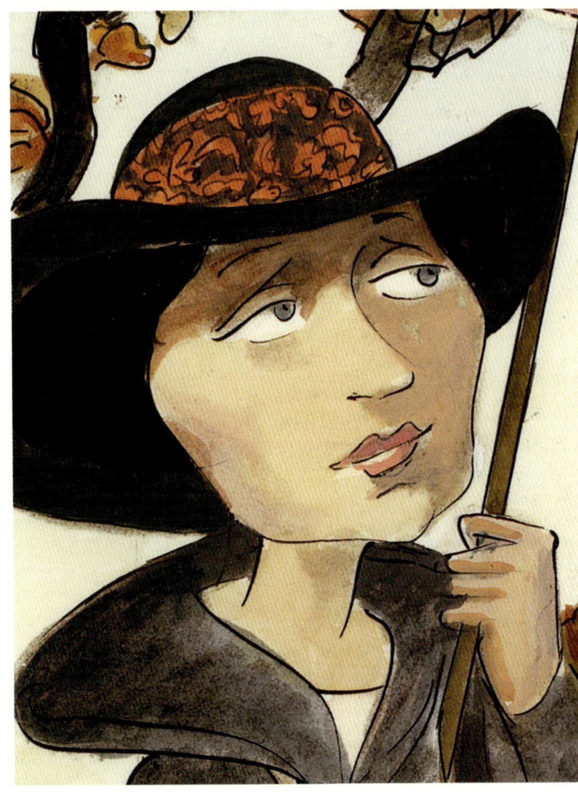

Margaret Sanger

MARGARET SANGER HAD A CAUSE. Everyone in the Village had a Cause. Everyone thought his or her Cause would change the world. Margaret's did.

Margaret expounded her ideas at Mabel Dodge's beautiful all-white salon, at 23 Fifth Avenue. This was where *le tout Village* came: Jack Reed, and Big Bill Haywood and Emma Goldman and Carlo Tresca, and Max Eastman. In her ladylike way, Margaret argued for the raptures of the flesh: sexual joy, without unwanted consequences. That was Margaret's Cause: birth control!

Margaret was trained as a nurse. She had seen desperate women in the slums. She wrote newspaper columns and pamphlets to educate women. She set up a clinic to dispense contraceptives. Soon, she was indicted for "obscenity." Margaret decamped to England, where she had love affairs: with the famous sexologist Havelock Ellis (who couldn't get it up) and with H. G. Wells (who could). Back in the Village, she founded the organization that became Planned Parenthood. She was often vilified, but there was no stopping Margaret's Cause. Margaret lived to see the Pill. And she lived to see the Supreme Court remove all obstacles to the use of contraceptives.

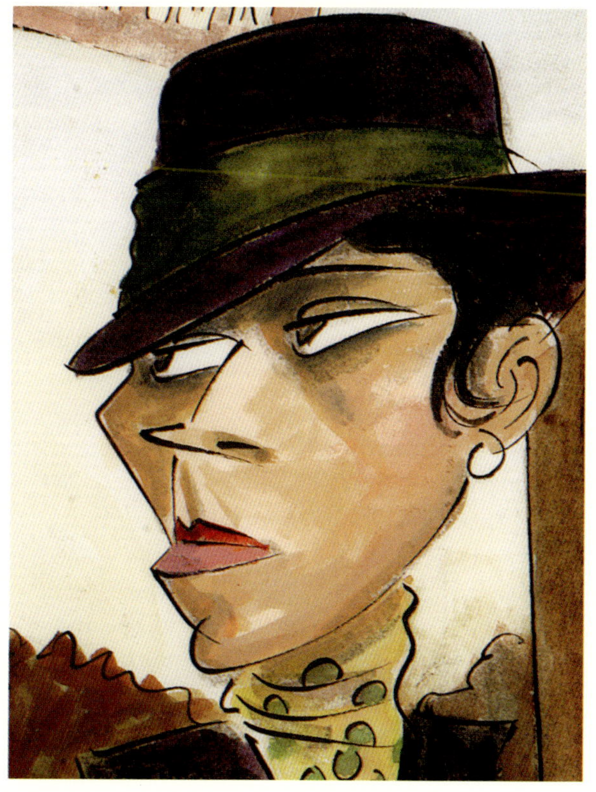

Djuna Barnes

DJUNA BARNES CAME TO THE VILLAGE in 1912. She was twenty years old, very tall and striking, and she caused quite a stir among men and women; in the arena of love, she sometimes did not trouble to discriminate between them. When it came to art, however, Djuna's standards were very strict. Edmund Wilson courted her but ruined his chances by praising Edith Wharton's work. Djuna preferred a modernist approach, as her own writing demonstrates. She also preferred Ernst "Putzi" Hanfstaengl to Wilson and became engaged to him. But Putzi left her for Germany, where he became Hitler's press agent. Mrs. Putzi is said to have saved Hitler's life.

Djuna moved to Paris in 1920, where she wrote for *Vanity Fair* and other magazines. She was known for her devastating wit and her black cloak, and she was greatly admired by James Joyce and T. S. Eliot. She and her lover, the sculptor Thelma Wood, drank and quarreled a great deal.

When Djuna came back to the Village in 1940, she moved into 5 Patchin Place. Djuna was wooed by Anaïs Nin and Carson McCullers, but she lived like a nun in her robin's-egg-blue room, until she died in 1982. Her ashes are scattered around the Village.

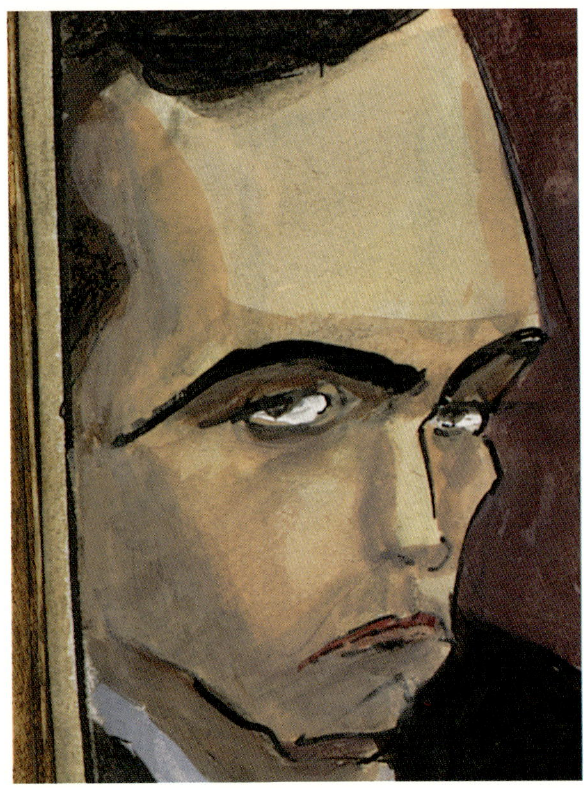

Edward Albee

EDWARD ALBEE WAS ADOPTED by rich folk. It is said that they paid $133.30 for him. The thirty cents seems a little odd. Whatever the price, Edward didn't get along with the Albees. He didn't get along at any of his expensive boarding schools, either. A difficult boy. A gay boy, it turned out. You would expect such a boy to head for the Village and write poetry.

A lucky boy. For when young Edward took his pages of poems and knocked on W. H. Auden's door, he gained entry. "Write pornographic verse," Auden advised, on the theory that it would sharpen Edward's skills. On the other hand, "Write plays," said Thornton Wilder, evidently not thinking much of Edward's poetry.

Edward wrote plays. Some of these, like *Who's Afraid of Virginia Woolf?*, brought him praise, fame, money, and prizes. Others brought down the wrath of reviewers, as when Philip Roth called *Tiny Alice* "tedious and pretentious" and "filled with ghastly pansy rhetoric."

Edward, admittedly, had some problems with alcohol. He has remained a difficult person. But he is not all that pretentious. For instance, when he was seated next to Johnny Cash at the Kennedy Center, he acknowledged that he had heard of the man.

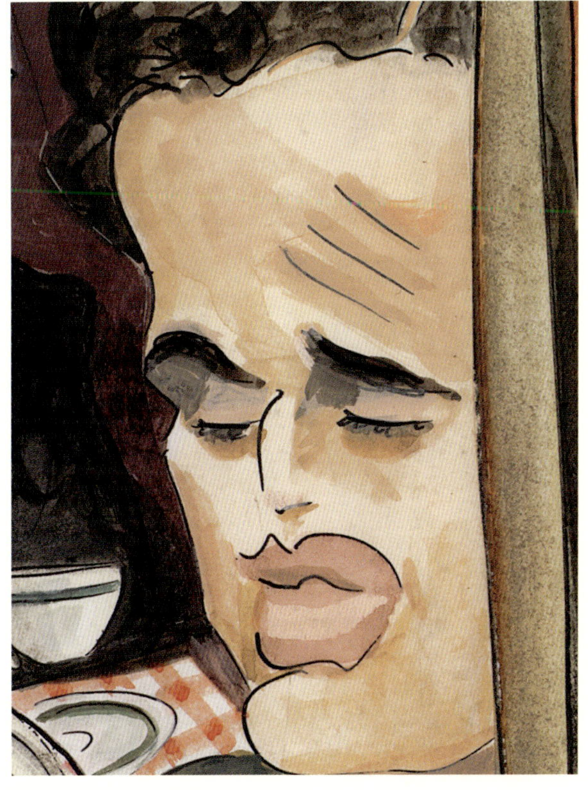

Marlon Brando

EVERYONE CAME TO THE VILLAGE. Marlon Brando came in 1943, but he didn't stay. His mother was an actress in Omaha, his sister was an actress in New York; Marlon was nineteen years old and a knockout. What else was he going to do?

Marlon studied with Stella Adler, with Lee Strasberg, with Sanford Meisner, with Erwin Piscator. He was a natural. Pretty soon he was on the stage in *I Remember Mama.* Then in *A Streetcar Named Desire.* Then he was in the movies.

Marlon made a lot of money in the movies, but he disdained Hollywood. When he won an Oscar for *The Godfather,* he sent a pretty girl, dressed in beaded doeskin, to refuse it for him. This was because of the way Hollywood treated American Indians. A little-known fact is that the girl, whose professional name was Sacheen Littlefeather, had previously been Miss American Vampire.

Women loved Marlon. He loved a goodly number of them and married several. He had many children, at least two of whom broke his heart. "I suppose that the story of my life is a search for love," he once said.

We can all identify with him there.

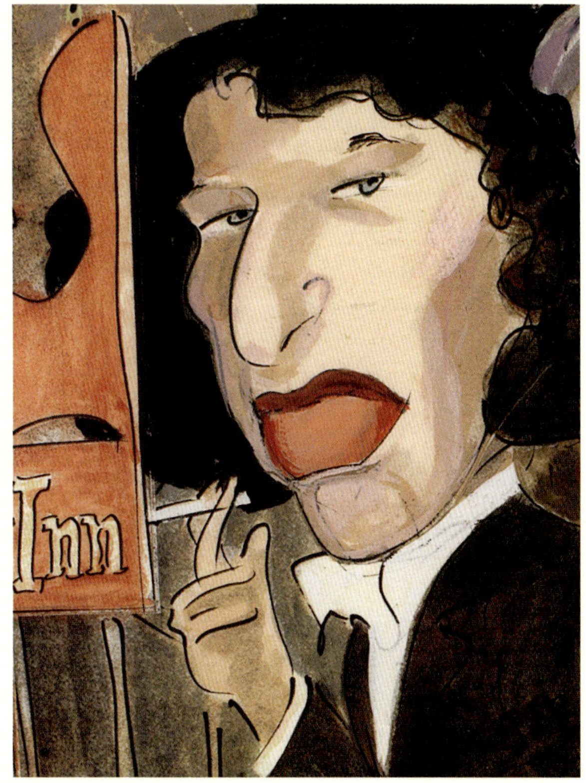

Fran Lebowitz

WHEN SHE WAS A GIRL in suburban New Jersey, Frances Ann Lebowitz was probably known as a smart-ass. Actually, she was trenchant. Soon she went to New York, where people understood her.

Fran wrote a column for *Interview* magazine. That was in the 1970s, when Andy Warhol's Factory was on Union Square, just across from Max's Kansas City. Fran honed her style and hung out at Max's. Fran believed in writing short; she believed that only a coal miner had a harder job than a writer. To illustrate her first point, she wrote two very short books. To illustrate her second point, she has been famously working on a novel for more than twenty years. People compare Fran to Mary McCarthy and Mark Twain, even though both of them wrote a lot more and faster.

Fran is famous for smoking and going to parties where she says many trenchant things about life. She is famous for sleeping. As she has said, "Sleep is death without the responsibility." Fran has also said that "spilling your guts is exactly as charming as it sounds." This is why, famous as she is, we know so little about her.

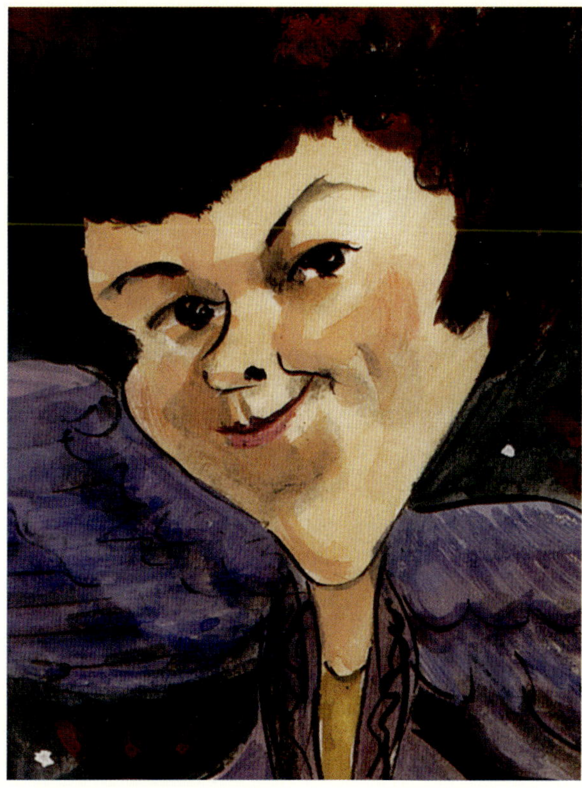

Dawn Powell

DAWN POWELL WAS AN UNHAPPY CHILD in small-town Ohio. She wrote stories and dreamed of New York. Soon Dawn was a published writer and living in the middle of the action. Dawn was no beauty, but she made people laugh.

Dawn wrote comedies of manners, lots of them: novels, such as *Angels on Toast,* short stories, book reviews, plays—also letters and diaries. Dawn was a true wit: "True wit," she said, "should break a wise man's heart."

Like almost everyone else in those days, Dawn drank too much. She gave many riotous parties in her duplex apartment at 35 East Ninth Street. On off nights, she held court at the old Lafayette Hotel, where her friends joined her. They included John Dos Passos, Gore Vidal, Djuna Barnes, Edmund Wilson, A. J. Liebling, Carlo Tresca, and so many more.

Dawn had money problems, she had problems with her husband, who also drank too much, and she had problems with her son, who was probably autistic. Dawn's last years were no fun. She was evicted from her apartment. Then she got sick with cancer. Dawn, like a character in one of her novels, took it on the chin: "She had learned long ago that there was no one on earth who could afford to weep, no occasion worthy of it . . ." Dawn's motto was *Allez oop!*

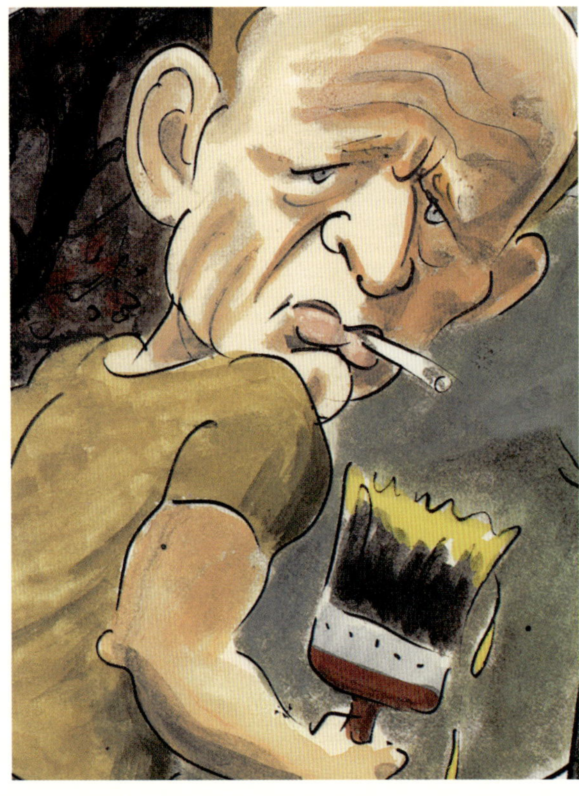

Jackson Pollock

JACKSON POLLOCK WAS EIGHTEEN when he came to the Village from Wyoming. The Depression had just begun. He lived all over the place: on Horatio, on Carmine, on Eighth Street. At first, Jackson painted like his teacher, Thomas Hart Benton, then like Picasso, and like Joan Miró, then like the Mexican muralists. When his crowd became the Abstract Expressionists, Jackson began to drip. Jackson wasn't the first painter to drip, but once he got the hang of it, he dripped more and better than anyone else.

There are always cranks who say, "I don't get it." But Peggy Guggenheim took Jackson up; Clement Greenberg became his champion; *Life* magazine asked, "Is He the Greatest Living Painter in the United States?"

When Jackson wasn't painting, he got drunk at the Cedar Tavern and got into fights. He was also known for his crudeness in propositioning women. In those days, if you weren't macho, drunk, and tormented, you weren't an artist. By those standards, Jackson was a genius.

Jackson married another artist, Lee Krasner. They moved to Springs, on Long Island. Jackson went on the wagon for a couple of years. But he was drunk the night he got into his car with two girls and drove into a tree. He killed one of the girls, too.

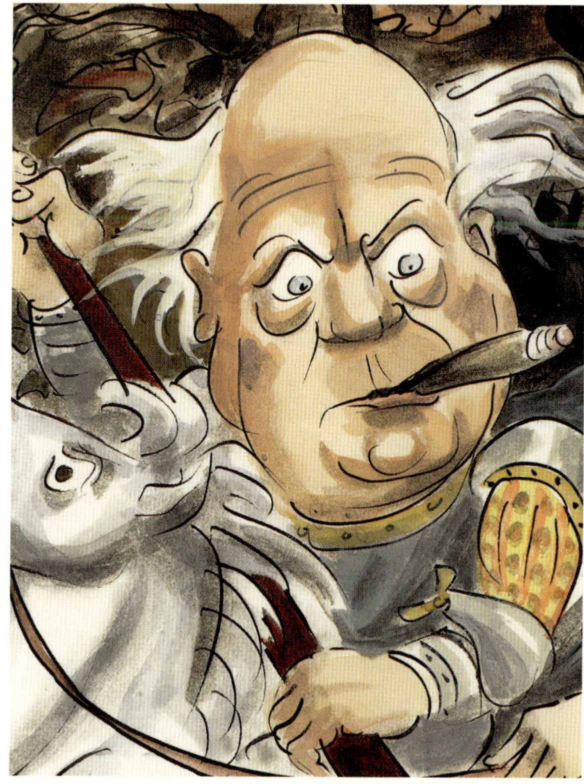

Art Young

ART YOUNG WAS JUST A FARM BOY from the Midwest. If he hadn't been given a book of Gustav Doré illustrations, he might have lived his life as a storekeeper in Monroe, Wisconsin. Art studied art in Chicago. He went to New York and then to Paris to study some more. At first Art drew anything newspaper editors asked him to draw. Then he got socialism and drew bloated plutocrats. He drew two children standing outside their hovel: "Chee, Annie," says the boy to his sister, "look at the stars. Thick as bedbugs."

Art was one of the founders of *The Masses* (91 Greenwich Avenue). Max Eastman was the editor. Every radical in America wrote or drew for *The Masses.* Nobody got paid. They did it for love. Art thought of his work as "savage assaults on every kind of organized meanness, cruelty, hypocrisy." Nevertheless, World War One came; socialism didn't. *The Masses* was suppressed.

After that, Art worked for *The Liberator,* for *The Nation,* for *The Saturday Evening Post,* for *Collier's,* for *The New Yorker.* He never made much money. In 1934, his friends held a benefit so he could pay his bills. When Art died in 1943, *The New York Times* condescended to him as "a lovable soul in spite of his sometimes heterodox opinions." He wouldn't have liked that, as *The Times* noted.

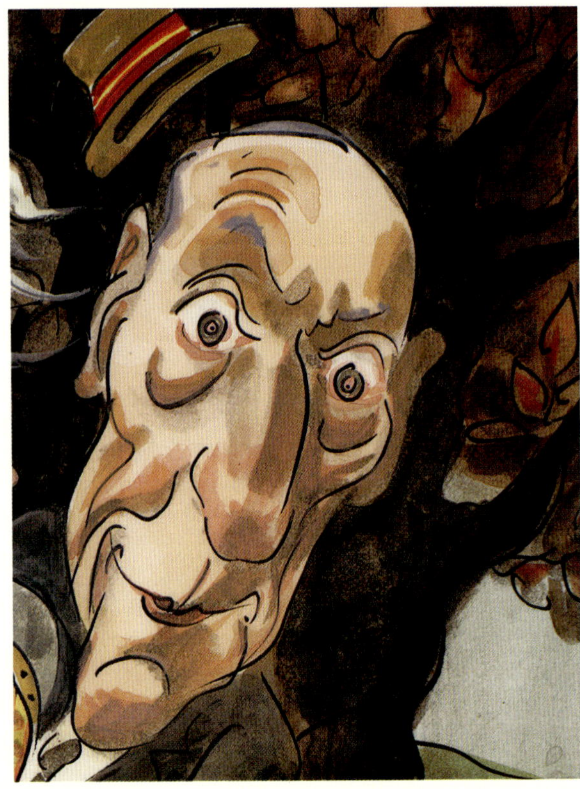

William Burroughs

BILL GOT AN ALLOWANCE FROM HIS FAMILY in St. Louis. This let him live pretty much where and as he liked. He liked New York, where he was a pal of Allen Ginsberg and Jack Kerouac. He liked Europe, where he cut off the last joint of his little finger to impress a young man he was courting. He liked Tangiers, where drugs were plentiful. He liked South America, where he went looking for a drug called *yage.*

In time, Bill had to flee New York for Mexico. This was to avoid an indictment having to do with drugs. In Mexico, while drunk, Bill inadvertently shot his common-law wife, Joan, dead. Ordinarily, Bill wasn't a lady-killer; rather, he was devoted to young men.

Bill's most famous book is *Naked Lunch,* which he produced by the "cut-up" technique; this involved cutting up the manuscript and putting different bits in different places. Not surprisingly, the book turned out to be nonlinear. Some people thought Bill was a genius; others thought otherwise. By the 1970s, Bill was a celebrity.

Bill always wore a hat, most often a fedora. Once, in Croatia, he married a Jewish woman to save her from the Nazis. In his diary, he wrote: "No one is perfect." In his own way, Bill was.

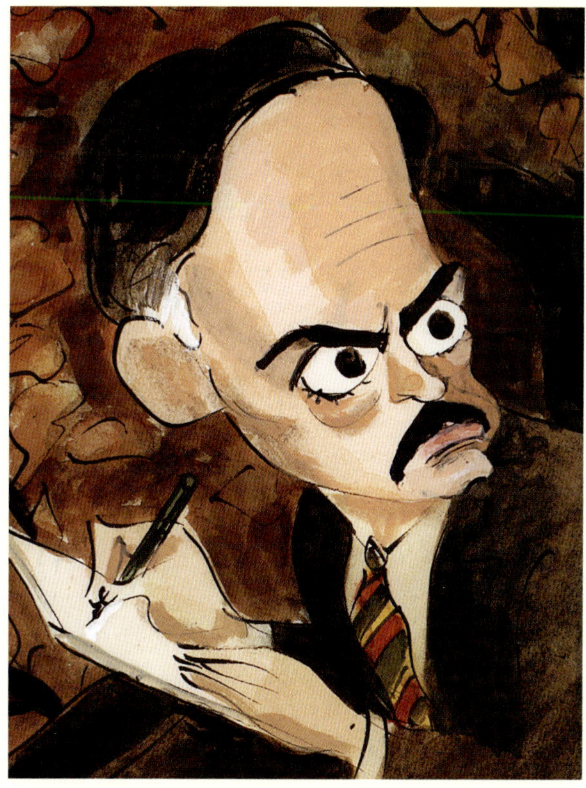

Eugene O'Neill

EUGENE O'NEILL WAS A GREAT PLAYWRIGHT. He was never more handsome than when played by Jack Nicholson in *Reds.* Gene's father was an actor, often soused; his mother became a morphine addict. Both parents were God-ridden. In discussions of Gene's work, his tragic view of life is often mentioned.

After being expelled from Princeton, Gene went to sea. Subsequently, he lived like a bum on the waterfronts of various countries. In his twenties, he started writing plays about lonely sailors, derelicts, and prostitutes. He was hanging around the Provincetown Players in the Village then; for a while he was in love with Louise Bryant, Jack Reed's girl, but he pooh-poohed all that revolution business.

Gene wrote twenty full-length plays in only twenty-three years. He won the Nobel Prize in 1936. He also got tuberculosis, attempted suicide, and married three times. Gene's two sons committed suicide; he disowned his only daughter, Oona, when she married Charlie Chaplin.

Gene wrote many cynical, bitter lines. But when he was young he also wrote this poem:

All night I lingered at the Beach / And trod the board walk up and down— / I vainly sought to cop a peach.

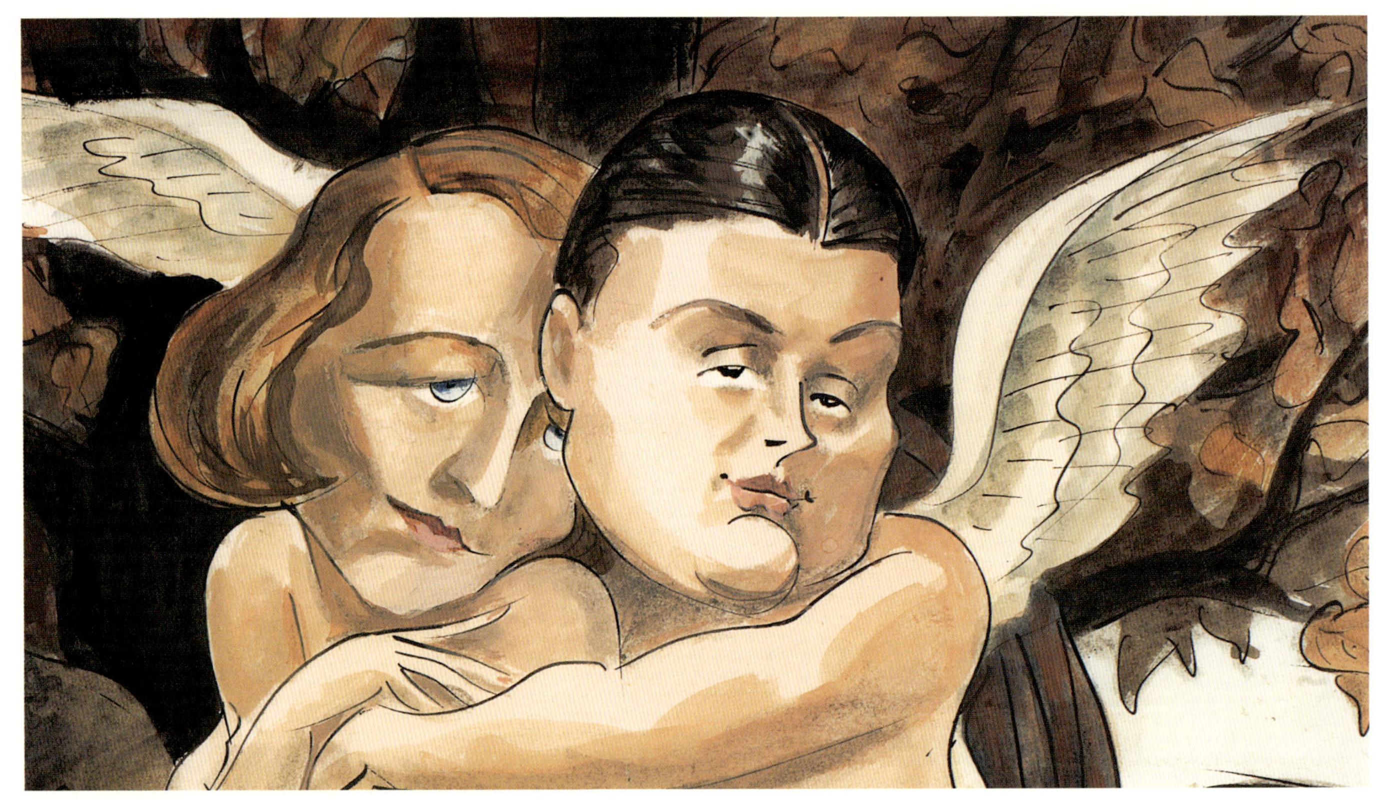

Edna St. Vincent Millay and Edmund Wilson

PEOPLE FALL IN LOVE WITH ME AND ANNOY ME and distress me and flatter me and excite me," wrote Edna St. Vincent Millay. Edna was a slender, ethereal, redheaded beauty. For a time, she burned her candle at both ends in one of the oldest and certainly the narrowest house in the Village: 75½ Bedford Street.

Edna was already a famous poet when Bunny Wilson fell in love with her. He was twenty-five and still a virgin; Edna, a few years older and very experienced, freed Bunny from his detestable condition. Bunny proposed marriage. So did Floyd Dell, at about the same time. Edna refused both but allowed both to lie with her, each gentleman entrusted with a different portion of her lovely body.

Bunny worked for *Vanity Fair* at that time and published some of Edna's poetry. She was the first woman to win a Pulitzer for poetry. Thomas Hardy remarked that America had two great attractions: skyscrapers and Edna's poems, which was even higher praise than the Pulitzer.

Bunny became a very famous writer and critic, the most learned in America. He wrote many books and articles, and he married several times. Mary McCarthy was one of his wives. Edna also married, on the understanding that her husband would not interfere with her love life.

The last time Bunny and Edna saw each other, youth had fled. Edna was heavy and dumpy; Bunny was portly and balding. Still: "The one train whistling in the afternoon silence . . . makes me think of Edna," Bunny wrote in his diary, recalling a summer day in 1920 when he took the train to Cape Cod to annoy and excite his lovely lady poet.

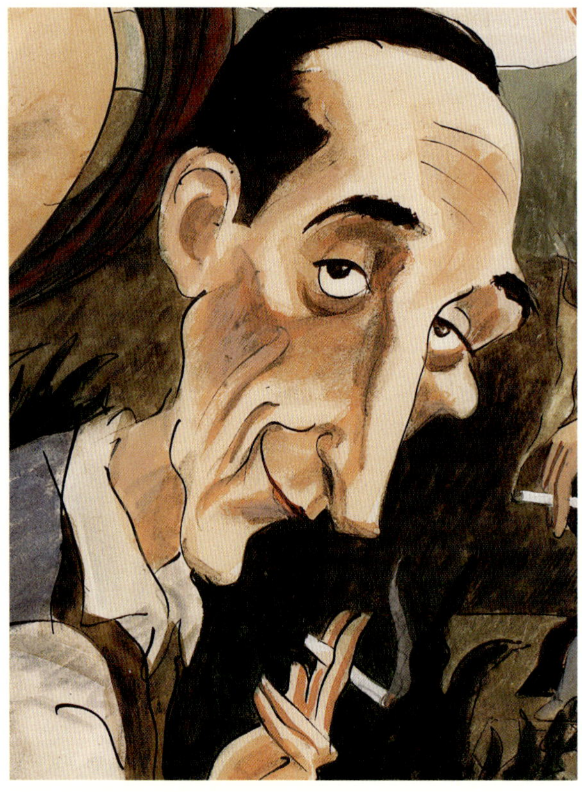

Marcel Duchamp

AT THE BIG ARMORY SHOW of 1913, Marcel Duchamp showed his *Nude Descending a Staircase.* A nude descending a staircase? Okay, if Marcel said so; modern art was what modern artists said it was.

Two years later, Marcel came to New York from Paris. Maybe Marcel was a Dadaist, maybe he was a Surrealist—whichever, Marcel saw art where no one had seen it. He saw a white porcelain urinal and called it *Fountain.* Why not? He saw a bicycle wheel, perched it upside down on a stool, and exhibited it. Why not? If it wasn't Art before, it was now. Or it was a Statement about Art. Marcel believed painting was finished. After all, could an artist make anything as wonderful as an airplane propeller, for instance? Marcel began exhibiting what he called "readymades." Today we call it Found Art.

Marcel settled in the Village. He caroused nightly with Man Ray and Francis Picabia; they all hung around Alfred Stieglitz's studio at 291 Fifth Avenue. After a while, Marcel stopped finding art and started playing chess. "I am a victim of chess," he said. "It has all the beauty of art and much more." In 2004, the Turner Prize committee called his urinal "the most influential work of modern art."

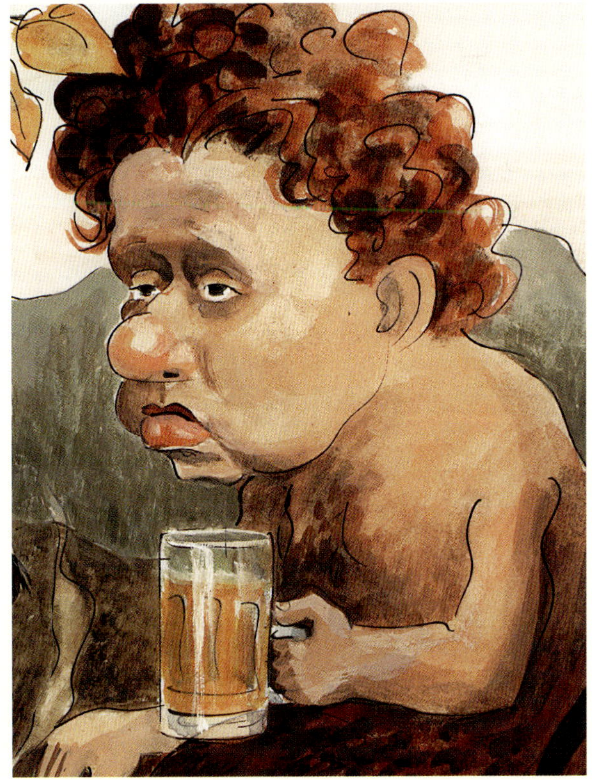

Dylan Thomas

FRIENDS AND ADMIRERS COULD OFTEN find Dylan Thomas at the White Horse. Dylan took breakfast there, usually beer. Morning refreshment might be followed by lunchtime brandy, with two raw eggs beaten in for nourishment. Then, on to the cocktail hour and whiskies through the evening. After that, Dylan might be off to an all-night party or, not very usefully, to bed with a girl. Dylan was a legend: no need to take that with a grain of salt.

Eventually, however, fewer friends were willing to put Dylan up for the night—the vomiting, the pilfering of clothes, so many requests for "loans." Then Dylan would sleep at the Chelsea Hotel, where, as the poet said, the cockroaches had teeth.

Dylan first came to America in 1950. His readings were swamped with fans, and he was paid pretty well. He came a second and a third time. The last time was in 1953. He was thirty-nine years old. That October, he read his great play *Under Milk Wood* at the 92nd Street Y. Huge applause all over town. By then, Dylan was sick as a dog: alcohol poisoning. In early November, his friends took him to St. Vincent's. Not unexpectedly, the light died.

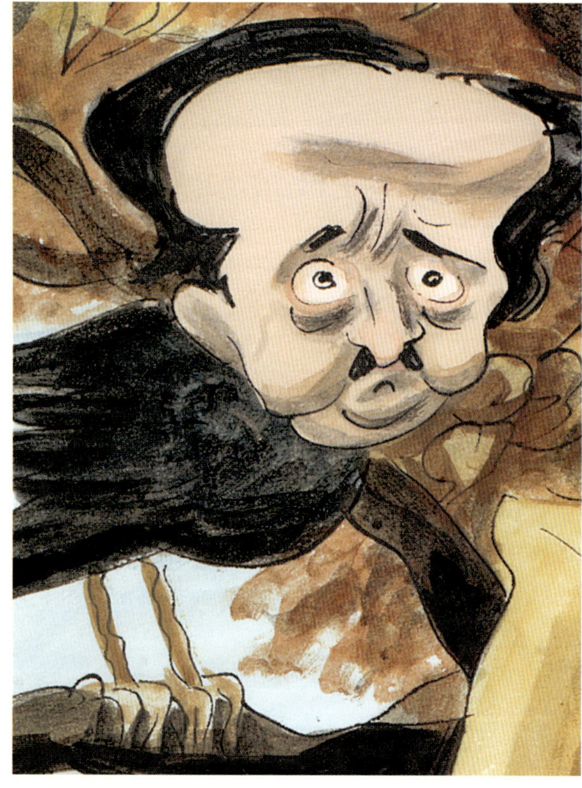

Edgar Allan Poe

FOR A FEW MONTHS IN 1844, Edgar Allan and his cousin-wife, Virginia, lived in a redbrick cottage at 85 West Third Street. Virginia was twenty-one. The Poes had been married for eight years. You do the arithmetic.

Edgar Allan was very productive on Third Street. He wrote "The Cask of Amontillado." At a nearby literary salon at 116 Waverly Place, he read "The Raven"; soon the poem was published, and Edgar Allan became an overnight sensation in America. And they loved him in France. This confirmed his belief that "o" and "r" were the most effective letters in the English language.

Edgar Allan turned his hand to everything: poetry, criticism, editing, essay writing; he invented the American detective story and the psychological thriller. But, oh! these artists with their depression, despair, drink, drugs, madness. After poor Virginia died of tuberculosis in 1847, Edgar wrote: "I became insane, with long intervals of horrible sanity."

"Deep into that darkness peering, long I stood there wondering, fearing." Two years after Virginia's death, Edgar Allan died, mysteriously, in Baltimore.

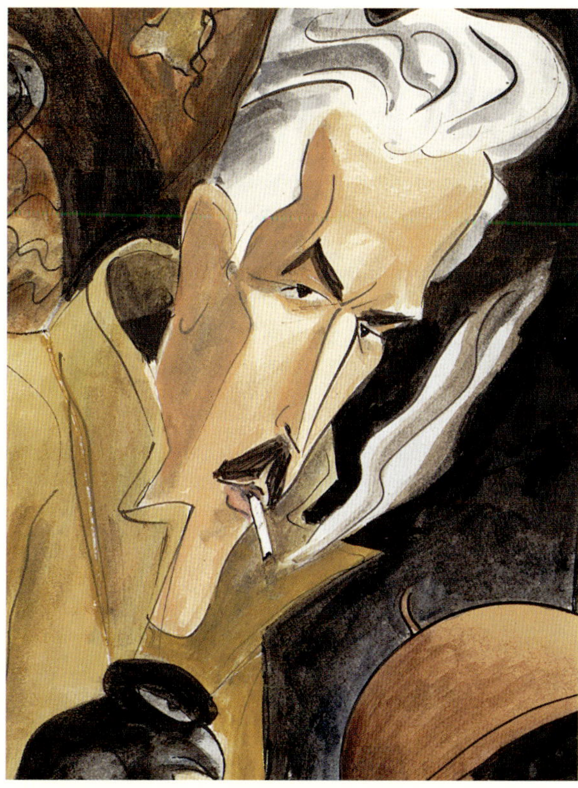

Dashiell Hammett

DASHIELL HAMMETT WAS A DREAM of a writer: tough, sexy, six-foot-one, silver hair, not an ounce of fat. He had a writer's résumé, too: newsboy, laborer, stevedore, Pinkerton. But he had some problems.

Dash wrote his five great crime novels between 1928 and 1935. Then he ran out of steam; he did movie work in Hollywood, did a lot of drinking and womanizing, and, oh yes, helped his girlfriend, Lillian Hellman, write her plays. All the time Dash was getting sicker from the TB he had contracted during World War One.

During the forties and fifties, Dash taught mystery writing at the Jefferson School (575 Sixth Avenue), a venue better known for courses like "Marxism and the Woman Question" and its companion "Marxism and the Negro Question." Yes, Dash was a communist. He spent five months in jail for contempt, when some communists for whom he had raised bail money fled without so much as a by-your-leave.

Dash got sicker. He had no money. Lilly had money, but she was known to be cheap (and, famously, to be a liar), but she did take care of Dash.

Dash knew, as he wrote in *The Maltese Falcon*, that "men lived only while blind chance spared them." He died in 1961. Lillian went on for quite a while.

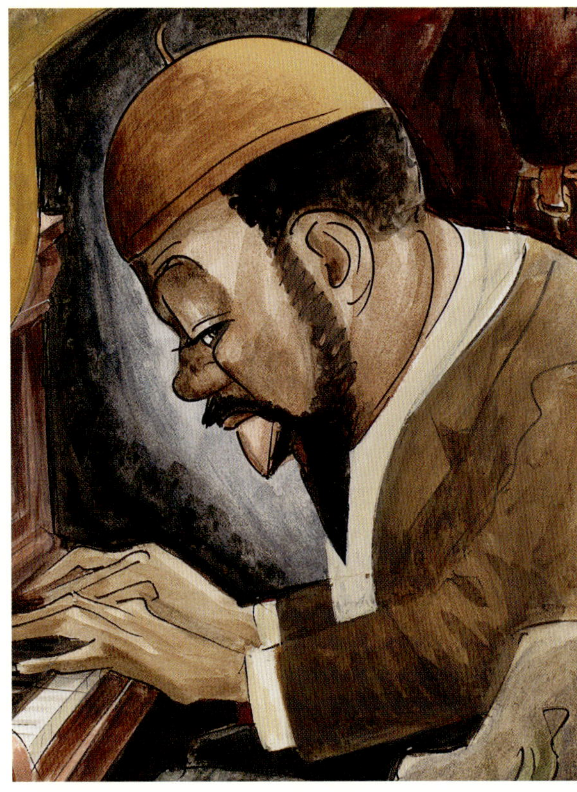

Thelonious Monk

THELONIOUS SPHERE MONK was his full name, a name as odd as his music, which critics lamely struggled to describe: “He does something strange” was the best one critic could do; his rhythms were “odd,” “awry,” “angular, “dissonant,” “not unlike the sensation of missing the bottom step in the dark.” But no one ever said Thelonious didn’t make an original contribution to jazz. And no one ever called him Felonious.

Thelonious went to Stuyvesant High School. He dropped out to play piano for a traveling faith healer. When they reached Kansas City, Thelonious met the jazz pianist Mary Lou Williams. She thought he was an extraordinary musician; later she said that seventeen-year-old Thelonious played the same way as a kid as he would for the rest of his life. His style was born in him.

Thelonious played with all the greats. He played with Charlie Parker and Dizzy Gillespie at Harlem jazz clubs. He played the Five Spot, the Village Vanguard, the Village Gate. He played the Newport Jazz Festival. He made many recordings. Often, when he performed, he wore one or another of his wardrobe of hats: baseball caps before they became de rigueur, coolie hats, berets, pork pies.

“Jazz is my adventure,” he said. He also said, quite mysteriously, “It’s always night, or we wouldn’t need light.”

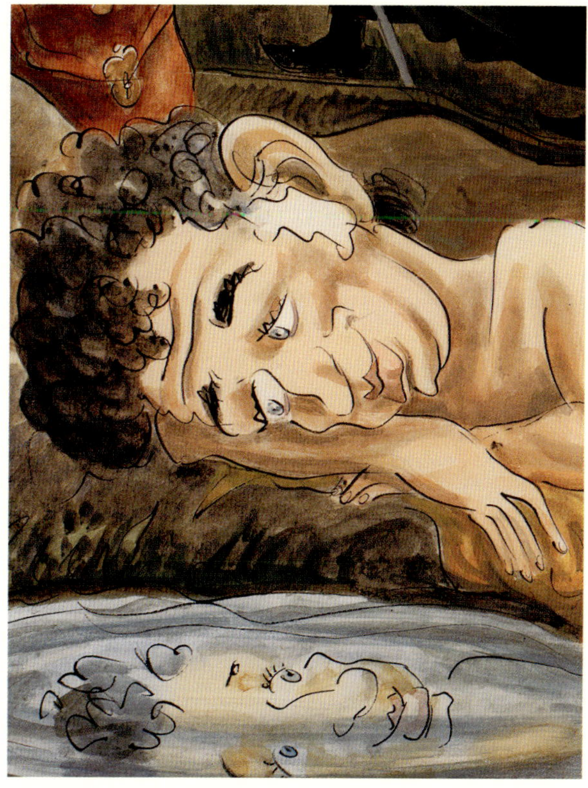

Norman Mailer

NORMAN MAILER WAS ONE of the founders of *The Village Voice.* That was a good idea. For more than fifty years, Norman was famous for other things: famous for writing books (dozens), for making movies (a few), for getting married (six times). For stabbing his wife Adele. Norman's mother was very upset by this. Why, *why,* does he marry girls who make him do these things? she cried.

Norman also ran for mayor of New York. He had many ideas about how he would govern: for one thing, the city would secede from the state, and each neighborhood would make its own rules. Not a bad idea. Later, he helped get convicted felon Jack Henry Abbott out of jail. Bad idea: once free, Abbott killed somebody. Norman publicly pronounced (controversially) on every social and political issue of his time; he had very strange notions about sex. He also opined (not necessarily admiringly) on his cohort of novelists. Woody Allen once claimed that Norman donated his ego to Harvard Medical School. Doctors are still dissecting that organ and are expected to issue their report in 2017.

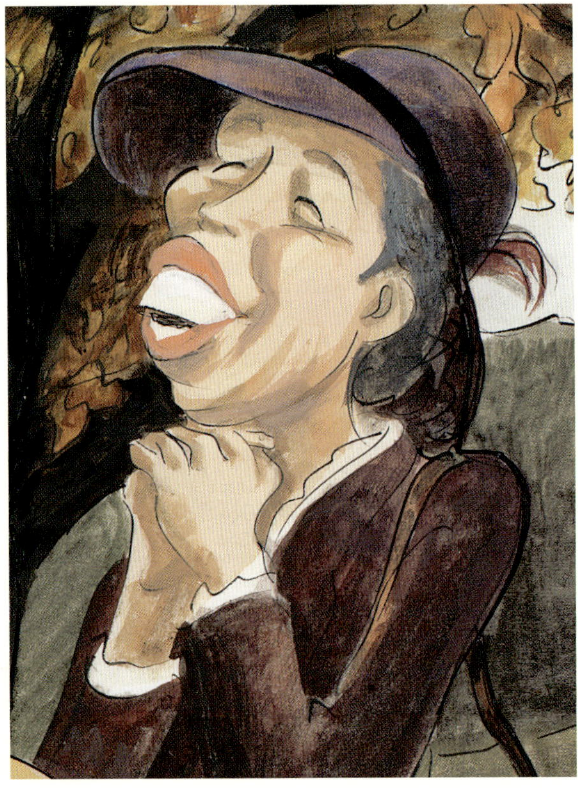

Eleanor Roosevelt

ELEANOR ROOSEVELT, poor little rich girl, was loved by her father, but he was a drunk and died young. He broke his daughter's heart. Eleanor's beautiful, highly social mother was deeply dismayed by the ugly duckling in her nest. And let's face it: while Eleanor had many assets—intelligence, a willowy figure, thick blond hair—she also had too many teeth and lacked a chin. (Crazy Joe Gould's pickup line: "You're the most beautiful woman I've ever seen, except for Eleanor Roosevelt.")

Then something extraordinary happened: Eleanor's handsome, rich, charming cousin fell in love with her. When Franklin became president, Eleanor learned to speak her mind in public, and this was brave because her voice was no pleasure. But Eleanor became a true political helpmeet. In those days, we really did get two for the price of one.

One day, Eleanor discovered love letters from her husband to lovely Lucy Mercer. Heartbreak again. But she had her work: to bring injustice to her husband's attention, which sometimes flagged, what with the war and all.

Eleanor had long kept an apartment at 20 East Eleventh Street. She loved the city. After FDR died, Eleanor moved to 29 Washington Square West. She parked her car in my father's nearby garage on West Third Street. Her old age was full of other honors, too.

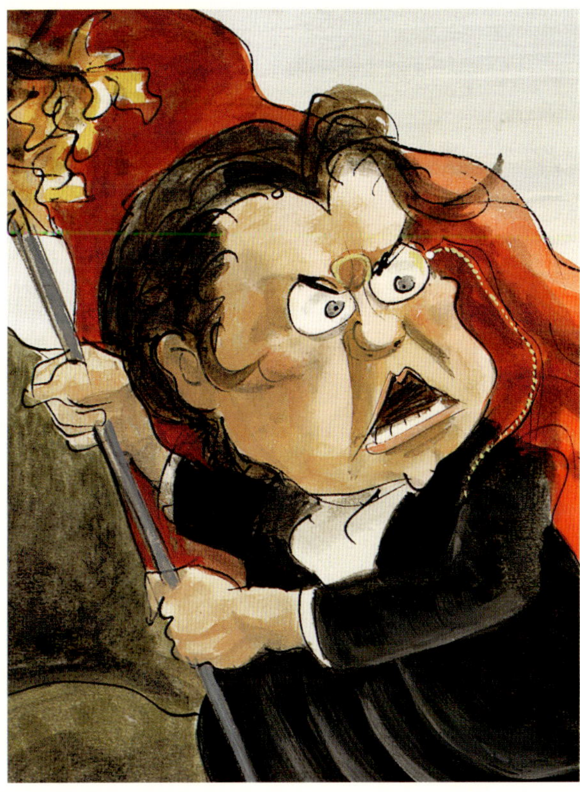

Emma Goldman

A GIRL FROM KOVNO FINDS HER WAY to New York with five dollars and a sewing machine. What does she make of the opportunities offered by the New World? She becomes the Most Dangerous Woman in America!

Living at 210 East Thirteenth Street, Red Emma published *Mother Earth*, espousing Anarchism, Atheism, Free Love. She loved Alexander (Sasha) Berkman freely. They believed in the "propaganda of the deed"; together they planned to assassinate the capitalist Henry Clay Frick. Sasha shot. Sasha missed the vital organs. He went to prison for fourteen years.

You could say that Emma and Sasha were terrorists when they were young. Later on, people who heard Emma lecture said she was more like a lofty scold. Meanwhile, alone in her room, Emma yearned for love and plenty of sex.

During the Red Scare of 1919, Emma and Sasha were deported to Soviet Russia; at least they would see the revolution made flesh. After a while, Emma thought she should have a little talk with Lenin. It didn't help. Then it was good-bye to the Soviet Union. Emma became a lonely wanderer, "cast out," as she wrote, "pursued by the furies and nowhere at home."

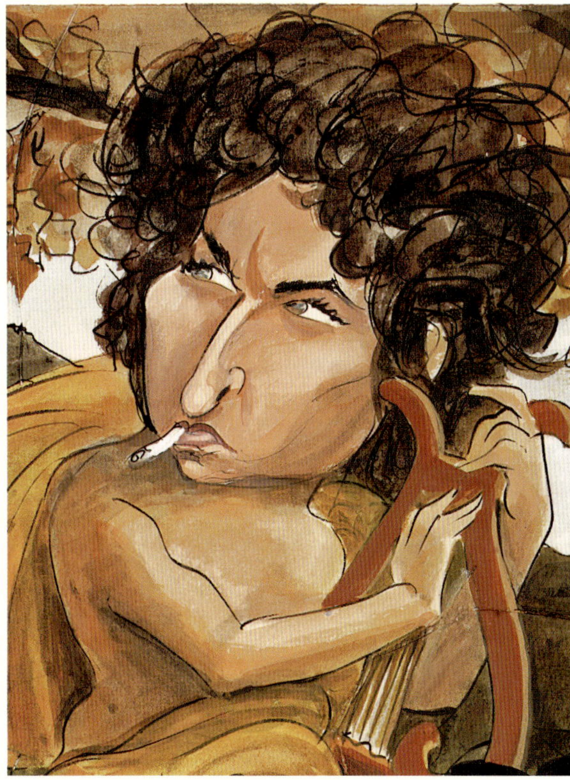

Bob Dylan

WHERE DO GENIUSES COME FROM? Sometimes from Odessa. Isaac Babel came from Odessa. So did Bob Dylan's grandfather Zigman Zimmerman, who carried his seed across the sea to Minnesota, where little Bobby Zimmerman was born. When the icy winds blew across the Iron Range, Bobby went to his room and listened to music on the radio. Bobby heard the call of the sixties. He came to the Village.

At first Bob imitated Dave Van Ronk and Woody Guthrie. But right away people heard something special in his nasal, gravelly voice, in the way he put words together. People were also impressed by his scruffiness, by his self-assurance, by his nerve to be, well, not very nice. For instance, Joan Baez fell in love with him. She invited him to sing onstage with her; this helped his career a lot. He never returned the favor; in general, he wasn't very nice to her.

Nobody in his generation became more famous, more emblematic than Bob. Professors of literature have compared Bob's lyrics, favorably, with Milton's. Allen Ginsberg wept when he heard his first Dylan song. Later on, Bob found Jesus, at least for a while. Apparently no doctrine instructed him to be nice. When asked what his songs are about, Bob said: "Some of them are about three minutes, and some are about five minutes."

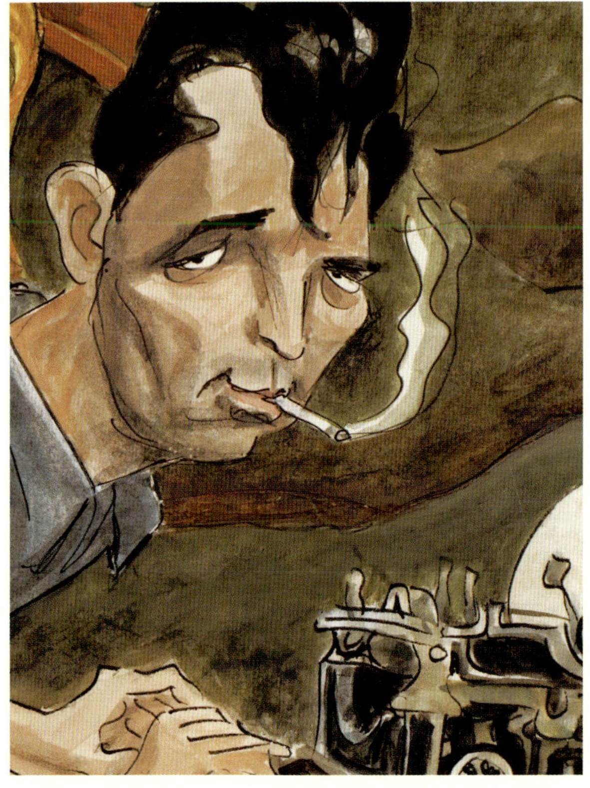

Jack Kerouac

IT WAS SAID THAT JACK KEROUAC wrote *On the Road* on a single roll of paper: type, type, type . . . smoke, smoke, smoke . . . no breaks except to light another cigarette. On hearing this myth, Truman Capote said, "That's not writing, that's typing." Truman's bile may be explained by the fact that some people thought *On the Road* was the masterpiece of Jack's generation, which, it so happened, was also Truman's generation.

Jack had thirty rules for writing. Number three was "Never get drunk outside your own house." Jack probably broke all thirty rules; he certainly drank at the White Horse, the San Remo, and wherever else he found himself.

Jack was very handsome, well-built, athletic; track and football were his sports. He got a football scholarship to Columbia University, and soon he met the rest of the guys who were to become Beats. He went on the road with them and shared their adventures and concerns.

Jack had girls galore. But the woman Jack really loved was his mother. He ended his short life with her in Florida, applauding the Vietnam War and drinking himself to death—in his own house.

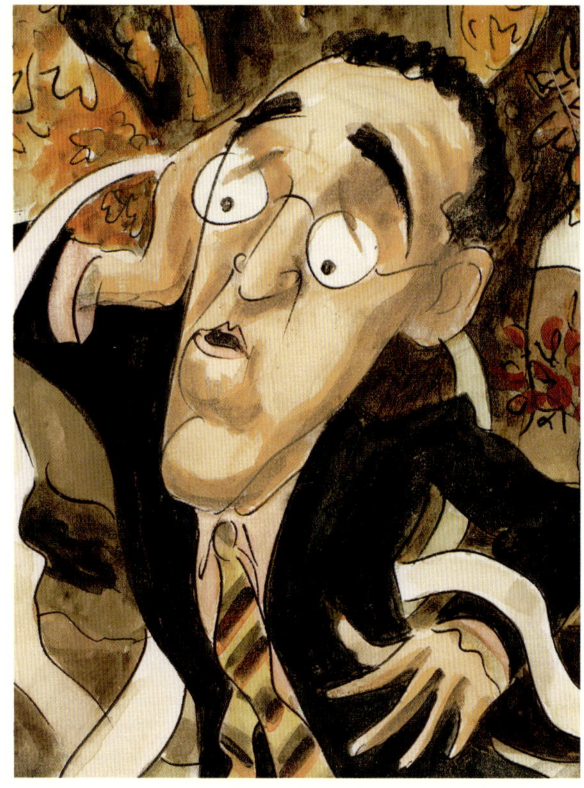

S. J. Perelman

S. J. PERELMAN OWNED SEVERAL lunatic typewriters, probably of the same make. He called Hollywood "a dreary industrial town controlled by hoodlums of enormous wealth, [and with] the ethical sense of a pack of jackals." He kept one typewriter in his apartment on West Eleventh Street, another at the farm where, as he said, he raised turkeys to display on Broadway (raising fowl was in S. J.'s genes; he grew up on a chicken farm), and a third to take on his travels, which he wrote about in *Westward Ha!* followed by *Eastward Ha!* However, Sidney Joseph (Sid) is best known for his feuilletons—little leaves—which he published in *The New Yorker* starting in 1930 and collected in books with titles such as *Dawn Ginsbergh's Revenge.* His lunacies include: "Just to indicate how cold it was, I left a tumbler of water at my bedside, and when I woke up it was gone." This was humor for intellectuals. Sid claimed James Joyce as a model.

Sid was married to Nathanael West's sister, Laura. He would be the last to deny that marriage prevented him from seeking feminine company. Nor would he deny that he was something of a grouch. "Home is where you hang yourself," he often noted.

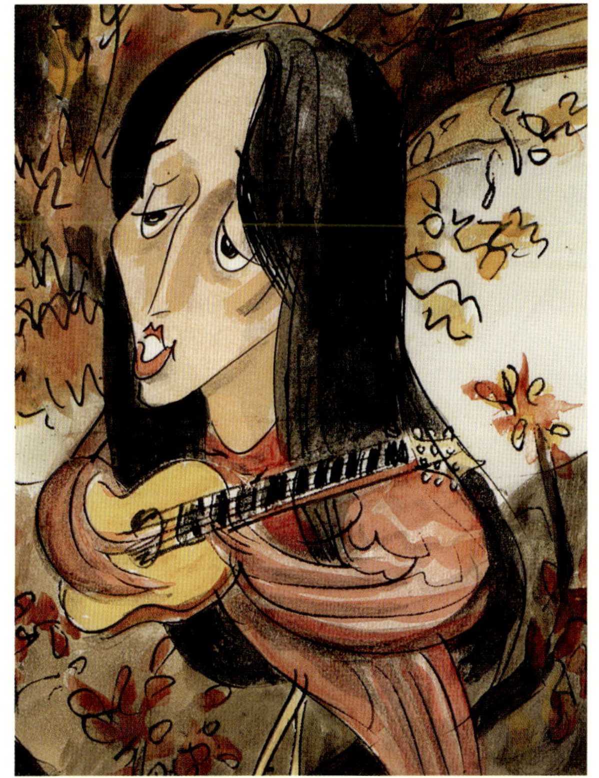

Joan Baez

IN 1961, BEFORE THE SIXTIES were the Sixties, Joan Baez came down from the Cambridge coffeehouses to sing at Gerde's Folk City on West Fourth Street. Everybody who would be Somebody sang at Gerde's. Beautiful, virginal Joan with her black curtains of hair, her pure, strong soprano—Joan was already Somebody. Right then and there she fell in love with a nobody self-named Bob Dylan, a scruffy footloose kid, not exactly clean, but, some kind of marvel. Bob already had a girlfriend; two or three, even. He gave Joan a hard time.

Joan had a huge career. She sang all over the world. She sang for all the right causes, like for civil rights and gay and lesbian rights, against the Vietnam War. She got married, but it didn't take. Years later, when she had cut off her long black hair, she wrote a song about a guy who had eyes bluer than robins' eggs; about a cold winter day when she stood with him at the window of a crummy hotel overlooking Washington Square. It was one of those moments when the world stops. *Speaking strictly for me / we both could have died then and there,* she sang.

This simply goes to show that once broken, a heart usually stays broken, but life goes on anyway.

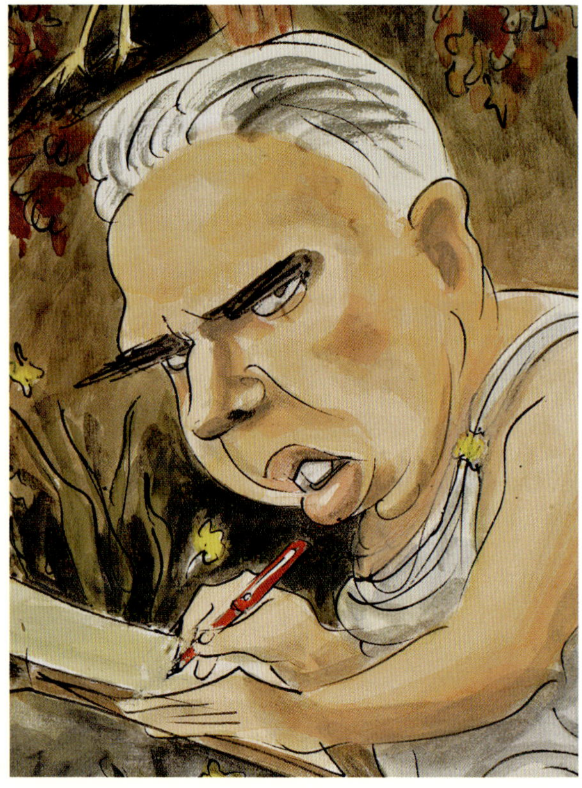

Theodore Dreiser

THEODORE DREISER WAS not a graceful writer. He was said to be the world's worst great writer. Neither in appearance (homely) nor in personality (sour, cold, and sometimes cruel) was he worth writing home about. "No more wit than a cow," said his Village neighbor, the editor Margaret Anderson. Nevertheless, Theodore was quite a stud. Fame helped, of course, but he found that relentless determination worked just as well.

Theodore first came to the Village in 1894, when he was a twenty-three-year-old journalist. In 1900, his *Sister Carrie* was published. But his publisher decided that it was immoral and refused to promote it. Theodore went into deep depression. This didn't stop him writing for long. He was living on St. Luke's Place when he wrote his masterpiece, *An American Tragedy.*

Theodore's nature and his life experience gave him a somewhat pessimistic view of the human condition. He believed that "all of us are more or less pawns . . . moved about like chess pieces by circumstances over which we have no control." By the time he finished his work, the Victorian novel was dead. His friend H. L. Mencken said that the novel before and after Dreiser was as different as biology before and after Darwin.

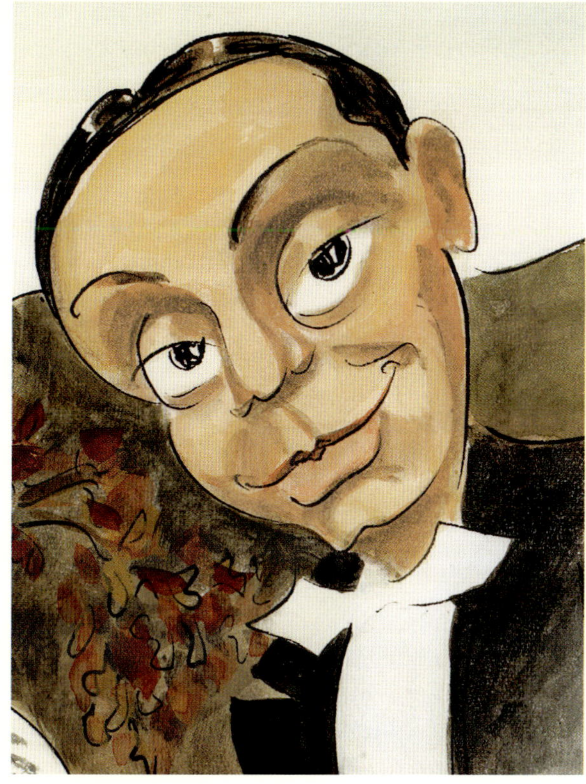

Cole Porter

COLE PORTER IS GREATLY ADMIRED. Of course. He was great. But the Village was never his style. He never lived in the Village, and if he came around, it was in a limousine, with a chauffeur to keep the motor running. *Why,* then, is Cole in this mural? Perhaps because he once wrote a song called "Washington Square"? Perhaps because the muralist's admiration ran away with him?

We must be satisfied with the following connection: Cole wrote the songs and music for *The Greenwich Village Follies of 1924*. This production played on Broadway, at the Shubert and Winter Garden theatres. It ran for 127 performances and starred the Dolly Sisters. Sadly, during the course of the run, Cole's songs were dropped one by one. By the time the play closed, not a single Cole Porter song remained. So, although people still hum "Night and Day," "Anything Goes," and "Let's Do It," nobody hums "The Dollys and Their Collies."

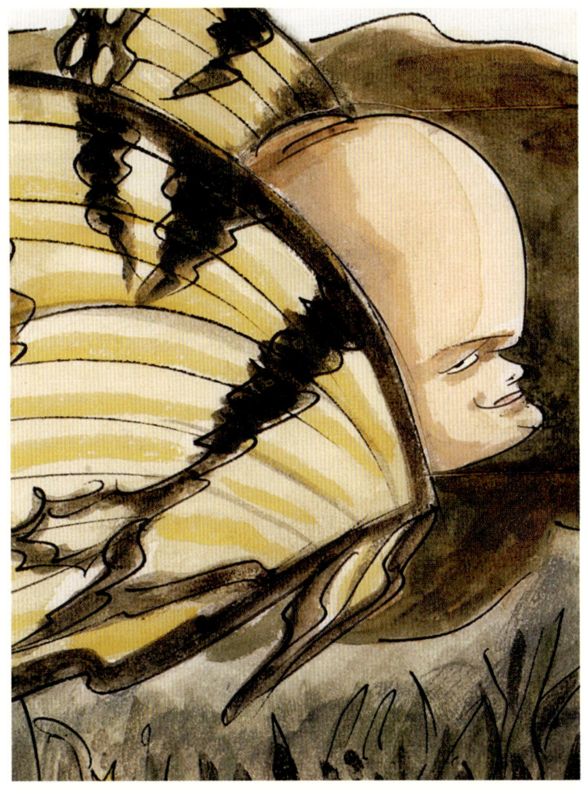

Truman Capote

EVEN IN THE SOPHISTICATED ENVIRONMENT of *The New Yorker,* Truman made an impression. One of his colleagues was startled to see a "gorgeous apparition, fluttering, flitting up and down the corridors." Truman was seventeen, with a menial first job at the magazine. He wore a black opera cape to work; his bright blond hair was cut into bangs in front and hung to his shoulders in back. New York is a designated refuge for strange birds, but no one had ever seen the likes of Truman's plumage.

And so Truman's career began: short stories, an O. Henry Prize, a novel. Truman worked hard, but he was distracted by celebrity. Dancing the night away with Liza and Andy at Studio 54; squiring Jackie's sister, the Princess Lee; cultivating his "swans," the ladies who lunched and told him high-society secrets. "All literature is gossip," as Truman knew. Eventually he told on the swans. It was his undoing.

In Cold Blood was Truman's masterpiece. When it was published in 1966, he threw the now legendary Black and White Ball at the Plaza. But, really, it was pretty much downhill from there. The sylph of a boy grew older, became bloated with drink and drugs. "Life," as he once said, "is a moderately good play with a badly written third act."

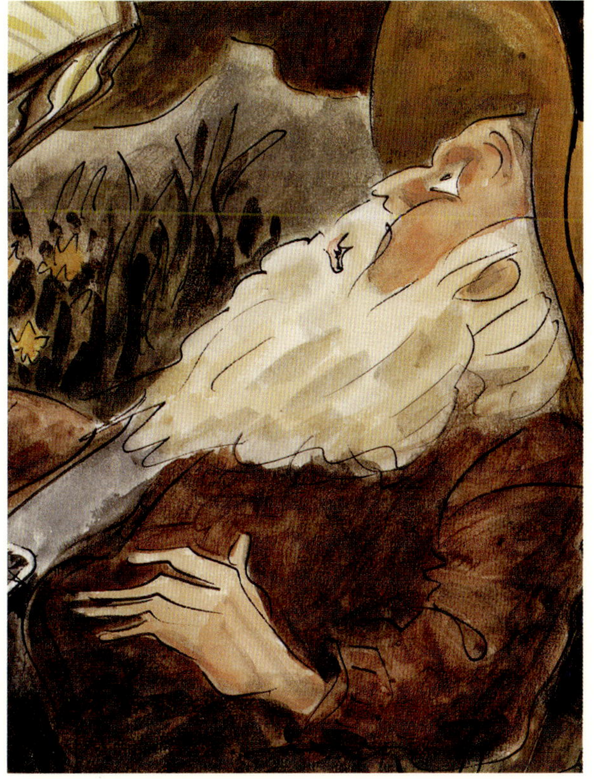

Walt Whitman

IN THE 1850S, WALT WHITMAN, poet and freethinker, frequently showed up at Pfaff's, a basement rathskeller, at 653 Broadway, near Bleecker. Pfaff's was the birthplace of our native bohemia. Actors, poets, singers, and painters gathered there. Walt was Pfaff's poet in residence. Walt had already self-published *Leaves of Grass*, the collection of poems he was to revise and enlarge as long as he lived.

Walt was born on Long Island in 1819, one of nine children in a Quaker family. After only six years of school, he was apprenticed to a typesetter, a trade that led him to an itinerant life as printer, journalist, editor, and poet.

Leaves of Grass was considered shocking and indecent in its erotic descriptions of the male body and of manly love between comrades. But it had fans. Ralph Waldo Emerson wrote to Walt, "I greet you at the beginning of a great career." And so it was to be.

Walt believed in America and democracy, but of course it was early days: Walt was only a generation removed from the American Revolution; he had walked the battlefields of the Civil War. If Walt wrote *"Rhymes and rhymers pass away . . . America justifies itself, give it time,"* we must remember that Walt died in 1892.

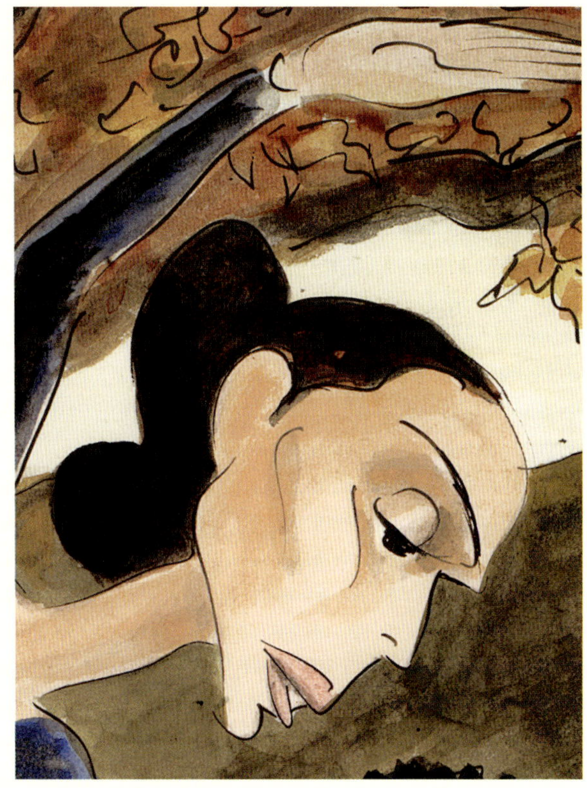

Martha Graham

MARTHA GRAHAM WAS VERY SERIOUS about modern dance. Her sacred mission was to express the "driving force of God that plunges through me." Martha was not the world's first modern dancer. First came Isadora Duncan and Ruth St. Denis. Not many people will tell you this, but probably first of all was Loie Fuller.

Martha trained with Ruth St. Denis's company. Then she came solo to New York, took an apartment in the Village, and danced in *The Greenwich Village Follies of 1923*. Soon Martha had her own company. Martha danced and danced and danced. At times her style could be somewhat overwrought. And Martha danced a little too long into her long life and became a parody of herself. But Martha's technique lives on in dance's common vocabulary.

Now modern dance can be anything, except for ballet, which brings us to Loie Fuller. Loie was a skirt dancer on the burlesque circuit; this was a technique of showing the body without actually stripping it. Artful movements combined with lighting effects on the dancer's voluminous, diaphanous skirt, and voilà! Loie was a particularly talented skirt dancer. Her technique, if not her name, lives on, too.

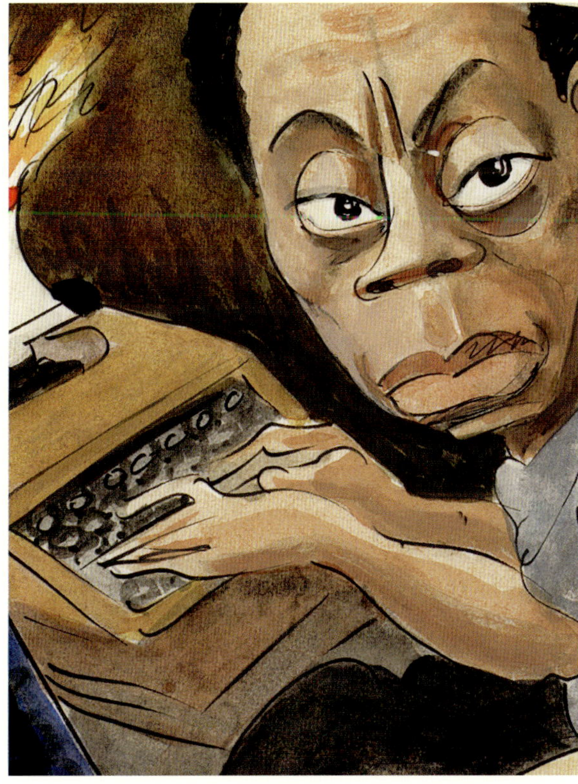

James Baldwin

JIMMY BALDWIN NEVER HAD AN EASY TIME. Poor, undersized, black, illegitimate, and, as it turned out, gay. Just for laughs, add a cruel stepfather. But Jimmy was a very smart kid. He preached in his stepfather's church, he graduated from De Witt Clinton High School. When he moved to the Village in 1944, Richard Wright took Jimmy under his wing. Then Jimmy criticized Wright's *Native Son* in print, and that friendship went south. Wright feared that the torch had been passed to a new generation.

Jimmy started his first novel while he lived in the Village. He wasn't happy in America and moved to Paris, then to Istanbul. He didn't come home until the civil rights movement began. Medgar Evers and Martin Luther King Jr. were his heroes. For a while, Jimmy was the most admired black writer in America; he made the cover of *Time* magazine in 1963. Jimmy could sound fierce. He wrote: "White Americans do not believe in death, and this is why the darkness of my skin so intimidates them." But Black Power was rising. To those guys, Jimmy was a pussy. They didn't like his homosexuality, his pacifism, certainly not his elegant rhetoric. Eldridge Cleaver said Jimmy's writing "displayed an agonizing total hatred of blacks." Once again, the torch had passed to a new generation. Jimmy went back to Europe.

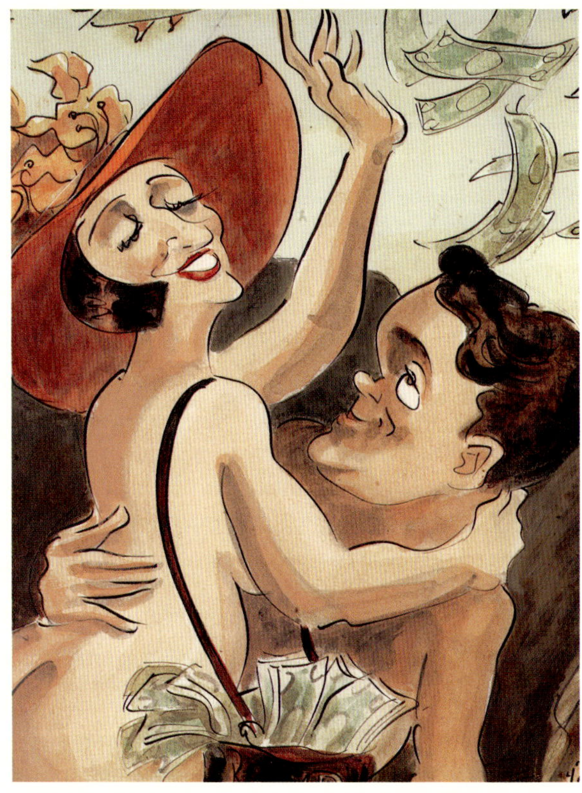

Mabel Dodge and John Reed

MABEL DODGE WAS A RICH LADY. She lived at 23 Fifth Avenue. She wanted to do something thrilling with her life, so she decorated her apartment all in white. Then Mabel had Evenings. She invited the "movers and shakers" of the day. There were burning issues to be discussed. As in every generation before and since, these issues concerned politics and sex. Mabel herself didn't have many opinions. To tell the truth, she was sort of a lump. She made the best of it by cultivating a mystical aura. But Mabel had a deep interest—spiritual, of course—in the orgasm.

One of her guests, Jack Reed, was not a lump. He was a radical journalist and very attractive. Soon Mabel and Jack were lovers. And soon, to Mabel's dismay, they were not. Jack had a world to change. With Mabel's tears still wet on his coat, Jack went to Mexico to write about Pancho Villa. He went to Europe to cover World War One. He went to Russia to cover the Bolshevik revolution. He became a communist. He married Louise Bryant. He died of typhus in Moscow. Mabel consoled herself by setting up a sort of artists' colony in Taos, where she married a local Indian and seduced D. H. Lawrence, much to his horror.

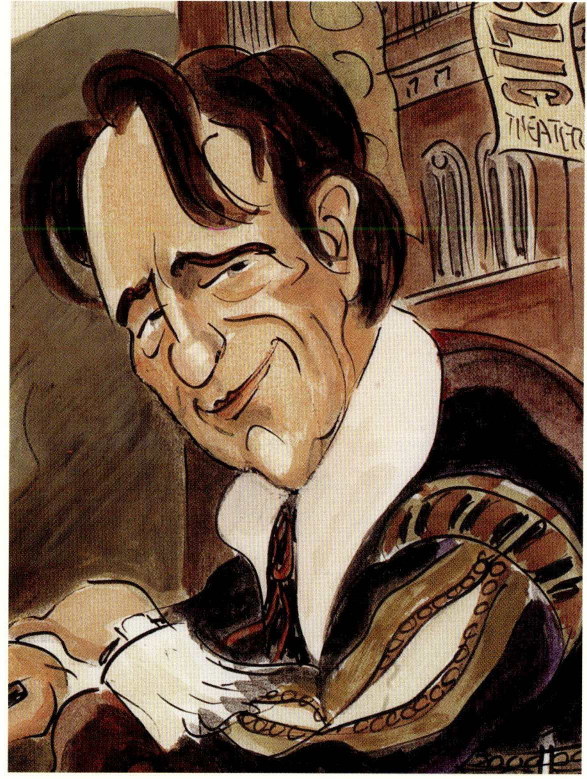

Joe Papp

WHEN JOE PAPP DIED in 1991, Broadway dimmed its lights. The theatre owed Yosl Papirofsky, Brooklyn-born son of dirt-poor Polish immigrants.

Joe had a high school diploma and the skills of a street fighter. Somehow he got the idea that theatre was "a social force" to which the citizens of New York were freely entitled. Robert Moses didn't see it that way. Joe fought Moses in the courts for the right to produce free Shakespeare in Central Park. Joe won. A few years later, when the beautiful old Astor Library on Lafayette was headed for the wrecker's ball, Joe got the city to hand it over to him. It became the Public Theater. Joe wasn't modest: "I am the most important producer on Broadway, off-Broadway—in the U.S.," he said. No one disagreed. Joe brought new playwrights into the theatre—Wallace Shawn, Miguel Piñero, David Mamet, David Rabe—and new actors, too: Kevin Kline, Meryl Streep, Colleen Dewhurst, George C. Scott. He brought Shakespeare to the streets of the outer boroughs and to schools. And he knew how to make money in the commercial theatre, too: *A Chorus Line* and *Hair,* for instance. Only a few hours before he died, Joe said, "My mind is teeming with ideas."

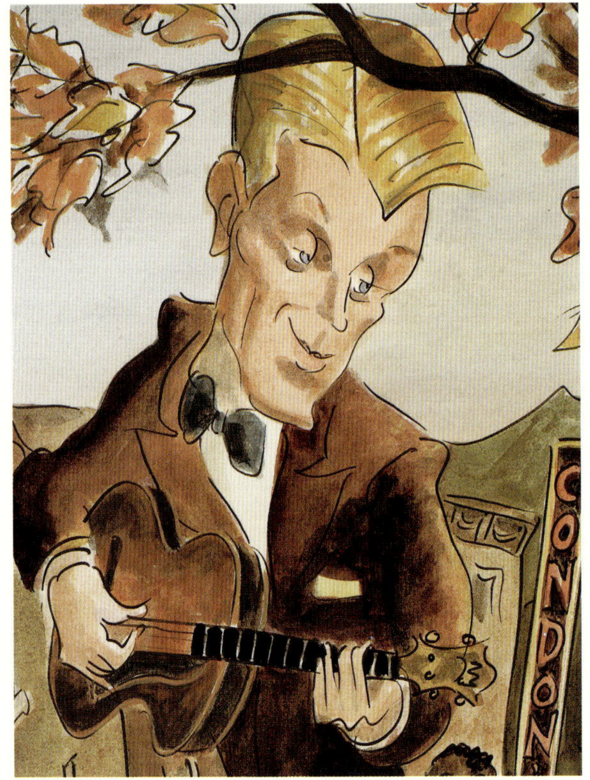

Eddie Condon

EDDIE CONDON HAD A CLUB. It was called "Eddie Condon's," and it was on West Third Street. After the war, and into the early sixties, anybody who wanted to hear Dixieland jazz went down to Eddie's club.

Eddie had a club policy: "We don't throw anybody in, and we don't throw anybody out."

When the club was too crowded, you could stand outside and listen to the fiercely rhythmic, hard-driving music spilling out over Third Street.

Before coming to New York, Eddie played jazz banjo in Chicago. In New York, he switched to the guitar, and played on Fifty-second Street and at Nick's in the Village. When he opened his own club, he insisted on mixed-race bands, which not everyone was doing in those days. Eddie had principles. Also, he wouldn't do a radio show when they wanted to add a comedian.

Eddie asked only one question when it came to jazz: "As it enters the ear, does it come in like broken glass, or does it come in like honey?"

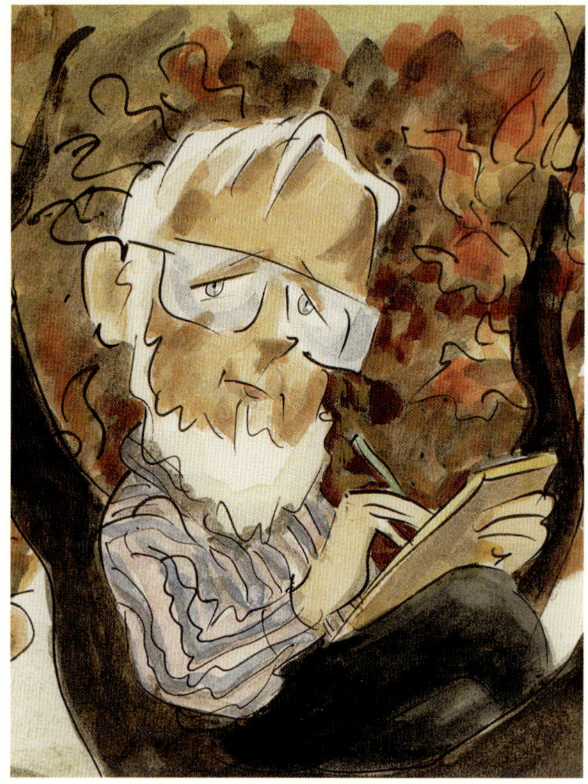

Donald Barthelme

DONALD BARTHELME CAME TO TOWN from Texas. He grew a beard (except on his cheeks, which remained bare as a baby's bottom) and plied his art on West Eleventh Street. Donald drank a lot every day. He had one wife, then two, and eventually four. He published his stories in *The New Yorker.* So far, so good; these are things writers do.

However, Donald was no ordinary writer. He was a postmodern writer. What is postmodernism? It's not Dickens, it's not Ernest Hemingway, it's not even Norman Mailer. Maybe it's Beckett, who was Donald's hero. Donald eschewed chronology, plot, and character; in fact, he eschewed the sort of writing that might be familiar to a reader from the experience of previous reading. Therefore, the question arose: Was Donald serious? Or was he, as someone said, a pretentious peddler of ironic word salad? Donald addressed this matter: art, he said, "is not going to be as honest as a mailman; it's more likely to appear as a drag queen." He also said: "I prefer the inane, sometimes. The ane is often inutile to the artist."

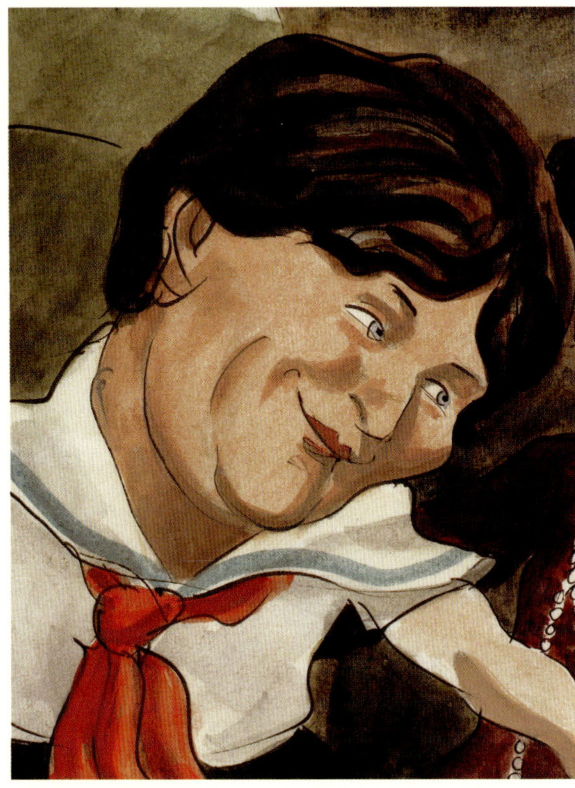

Willa Cather

WILLA CATHER CAME TO NEW YORK in 1906 to work on *McClure's* magazine. Willa was thirty-three years old, plain, foursquare, on the dowdy side, and already a writer. Willa first lived in a studio apartment at 60 Washington Square South. When she quit her job to write full-time, she found a nice sunny apartment at 5 Bank Street—seven rooms, forty-two dollars per month, if you can believe that.

Willa shopped at the Jefferson Market, ate at the Brevoort Hotel, and on sunny days could be seen reading on a bench in Washington Square Park. Yes, Willa was in the Village, but not of it. Willa did not care for bohemian goings-on—the parties, the drinking, all that noisy free love. Willa liked her privacy. "To love aloud is often to love amiss," as Swinburne wrote and Willa noted. Willa needed a quiet domestic life. She wanted to write and to travel. Edith Lewis was Willa's companion for many years. She ran Willa's household and took care of all Willa's needs, maybe even sex. Only they ever knew for sure.

By the middle of the 1920s, Willa's novels had made her famous all over the world. Today, she is in the canon. "The business of an artist's life," she once wrote, "is not Bohemianism . . . but ceaseless and unremitting labor."

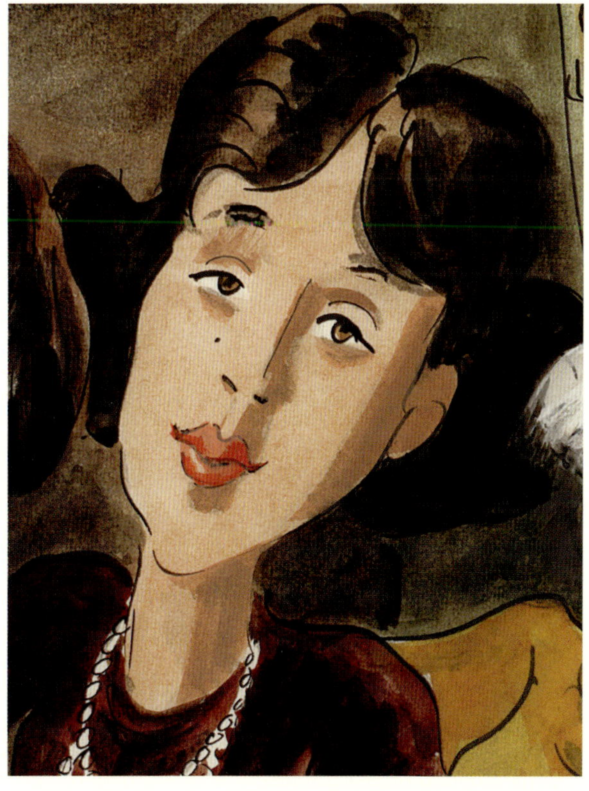

Gertrude Vanderbilt Whitney

AS A NATION OF ART LOVERS, we are in debt to Gertrude Vanderbilt Whitney, who gave us the Whitney Museum of American Art. Indirectly, we owe her for designer jeans.

Gertrude was born very rich. She married very rich. Gertrude was beautiful and sensitive to beauty. She went to Europe, where she collected art. She became a sculptor herself. In 1931, she founded the Whitney Museum, which was first located at 8–14 West Eighth Street.

As for the jeans, they came to us via Gertrude's niece Gloria. Gertrude thought little Gloria was being badly brought up. So she sued little Gloria's mother and won custody of little Gloria. Little Gloria was traumatized and confused. This may be why she eventually rented out her name to be embroidered on the back pocket of some jeans. Thus, designer jeans! What an idea! Isn't it possible that if Gertrude had minded her own business, little Gloria would have found some other way to make her mark in the world, and that poor people, for whom jeans had been intended in the first place, would still be able to afford them? So to Gertrude we say, thanks a lot, and thanks a lot!

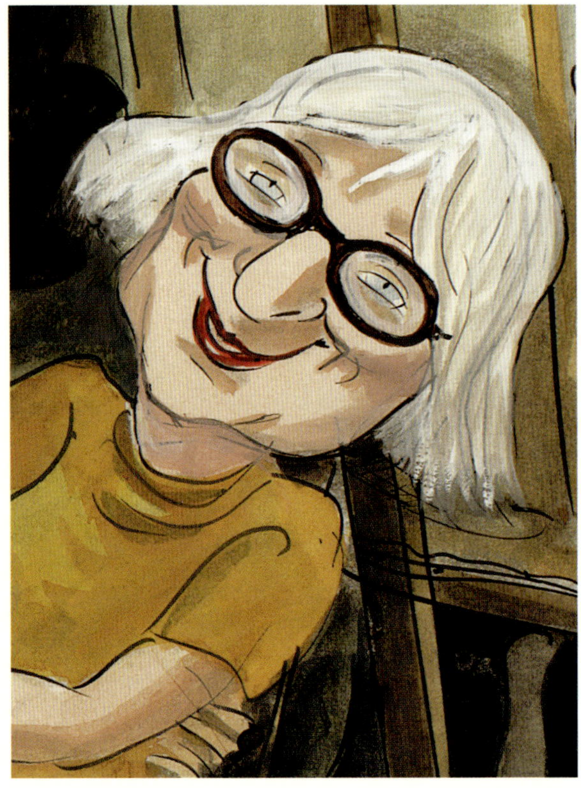

Jane Jacobs

THE MEN IN CHARGE OF NEW YORK CITY had a plan: label certain neighborhoods slums, bulldoze them, and call it "slum clearance." Let real-estate developers build high-rises and call that "urban renewal." Also, bulldoze entire historic districts and cover them with expressways. Robert Moses was devoted to the expressway.

Jane Jacobs lived above a candy store at 555 Hudson Street, near the White Horse, where she liked to have a beer. Jane knew that people didn't like to live in isolated high-rises. They liked to be close to one another and to the street. They liked to keep an eye on their children at play, to go to the local shoemaker, to chat with their neighbors on the stoop. Jane wrote a great book, *The Death and Life of Great American Cities.* She organized people to make a fuss. She helped stop Moses's Lower Manhattan Expressway. Jane was called names and was arrested a couple of times, but, as Napoleon observed, "no plan has ever survived contact with the enemy." Our Jane was the enemy. She saved the Village.

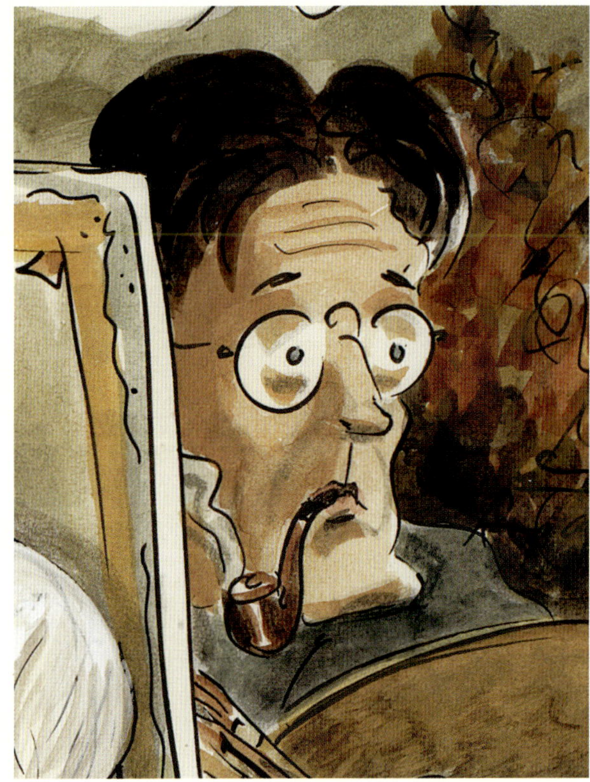

John Sloan

JOHN SLOAN WAS A PAINTER WHO LOVED New York as only a boy from a small town in Pennsylvania could love it. He painted the El curving around the Flatiron Building in a winter sunset; he painted the Jefferson Market from his window at 88 Washington Place; he painted McSorley's; he painted the Staten Island ferry in a heavy sea. His paintings are so beautiful they break your heart.

John had a social conscience. He joined the Socialist Party and drew for *The Masses,* illustrating the injustices of capitalism. For these drawings, he became known as the American Hogarth. John was one of the eight artists known as the Ashcan School, for the realism of their urban landscapes.

More than politics (though not as much as his wife, Dolly), John loved art. "Though a living cannot be made at art, art makes life worth living," he wrote. But art changed. People like Franz Kline, who had been influenced by John, began to make abstract paintings. John wanted to go where art was going. He couldn't go there. That probably broke his heart.

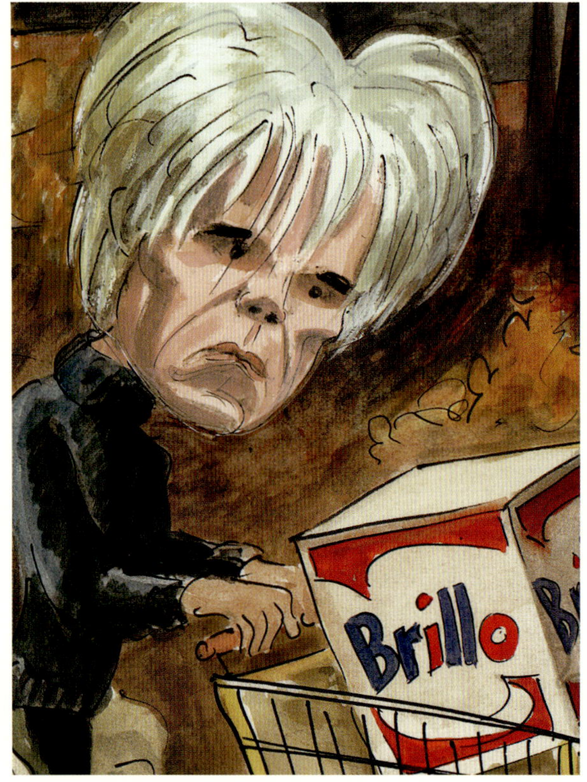

Andy Warhol

ANDY WARHOL WAS SO FAMOUS that no more need be said about him here. Although we might mention how much the Abstract Expressionists hated him. They spend their lives struggling for self-expression with paint. Along comes Andy. He buys a few items from the grocery store and right away he's a "blazingly" original artist. Yes. Well. What is art when it's exactly the same as a Brillo box? And why does one cost so much more than the other? Andy's art raised these deep philosophical questions. Of course, Marcel Duchamp had already raised these questions.

For many years, Andy turned out his work at The Factory on Union Square. That's where he made lots of his art and his films. (One of his best films is of the Empire State Building. Just standing there. For eight hours.) Also, The Factory is where he got shot by Valerie Solanas, founder and lone member of the Society for Cutting Up Men.

Andy loved being rich and famous. He loved one-named people like Liza and Bianca and Viva and Edie. But was he happy? Andy suffered from a bad complexion and thinning hair, which might be why he said, "Being born is like being kidnapped. And then sold into slavery."